ROUTLEDGE LIBRARY EDITIONS:
W. B. YEATS

I0585612

Volume 2

W. B. YEATS AND
T. STURGE MOORE

W. B. YEATS AND T. STURGE MOORE

Their Correspondence
1901–1937

Edited by
URSULA BRIDGE

Routledge
Taylor & Francis Group

LONDON AND NEW YORK

First published in 1953 by Routledge & Kegan Paul Ltd

This edition first published in 2017
by Routledge
2 Park Square, Milton Park, Abingdon, Oxon OX14 4RN

and by Routledge
711 Third Avenue, New York, NY 10017

Routledge is an imprint of the Taylor & Francis Group, an informa business

© 1953 Ursula Bridge

All rights reserved. No part of this book may be reprinted or reproduced or utilised in any form or by any electronic, mechanical, or other means, now known or hereafter invented, including photocopying and recording, or in any information storage or retrieval system, without permission in writing from the publishers.

Trademark notice: Product or corporate names may be trademarks or registered trademarks, and are used only for identification and explanation without intent to infringe.

British Library Cataloguing in Publication Data
A catalogue record for this book is available from the British Library

ISBN: 978-1-138-21351-7 (Set)
ISBN: 978-1-315-44820-6 (Set) (ebk)
ISBN: 978-1-138-68760-8 (Volume 2) (hbk)
ISBN: 978-1-138-68761-5 (Volume 2) (pbk)
ISBN: 978-1-315-54223-2 (Volume 2) (ebk)

Publisher's Note
The publisher has gone to great lengths to ensure the quality of this reprint but points out that some imperfections in the original copies may be apparent.

Disclaimer
The publisher has made every effort to trace copyright holders and would welcome correspondence from those they have been unable to trace.

W. B. Yeats at the Abbey Theatre (1932)

W. B. YEATS
AND T. STURGE MOORE

Their Correspondence

1901-1937

Edited by
URSULA BRIDGE

ROUTLEDGE & KEGAN PAUL LTD

Broadway House, 68-74 Carter Lane

London

First published in 1953
by Routledge & Kegan Paul Ltd
Broadway House, 68-74 Carter Lane
London, E.C.4
Printed in Great Britain
by T. and A. Constable Ltd
Edinburgh

CONTENTS

ILLUSTRATIONS

T. Sturge Moore at Torre Pellice (about 1926)

INTRODUCTION

THE TWO POETS whose correspondence forms this book, Thomas Sturge Moore (1870-1944) and William Butler Yeats (1865-1939), met through a third poet, Laurence Binyon, two years before the new century and formed a friendship that lasted until Yeats died. Looking back through the years, Sturge Moore wrote of the first meeting and the dual effect Yeats had on him: 'His derision of the puritanical and scientific bases of my bringing up roused me to contend as much as his witty dream-soaked talk delighted me. . . . I had early waited for a Leonardesque sweetness and subtlety which visited his features, and even in his bulky latter-day impressiveness sometimes refound it. . . . He was fascinating both to watch and listen to; I liked him best alone; then the provocative truculence of his talk often gave place to seductive delicacy.' (*English:* Summer 1939.) Yeats left no comparable description of Sturge Moore but much of this poet's character is seen by reflection in his brother's sedate and captivating autobiographical note to *The Philosophy of G. E. Moore* (Library of Living Philosophers, Northwestern University 1942).

In the early days Yeats and Sturge Moore often saw each other in London where both played active parts in the literary and artistic scene—a scene crowded with the many well-known figures of the Nineties and of the Edwardian era and lit by a concentrated brilliance that, apart from the measuring of talent, astonishes those standing in the pale wide dissipated light of today. Later on Yeats lived chiefly in Ireland, while Sturge Moore spent much time in the country and abroad, so they met less often but kept in touch by letter. Fortunately some record of forty years of friendship has been preserved.

Perhaps the rule about reading other people's letters applies also to the dead and the famous; perhaps they should be judged on their work only. The person who thinks so may be tinged with intellectual priggishness but he will study literature seriously and without preconceived ideas, and he will leave himself a new and delightful world to be discovered later on at temptation's touch. Certainly the letters and the details of a writer's private life are more safely studied after his work, when instead of limiting a poem or prose composition by too close an identification with actual fact they may add interest and help the critic to appreciate and evaluate it. If the critic is also to understand something of the mind and character of the writer, the nature of the man in relation to but distinct from his work, then, since creative activity throws shadow as well as light, the letters must be read.

It will not be necessary to say much here about Yeats. He has long been famous. The greater part of his letters are still unpublished but much is known of him without them. Much he told himself, not always in the way least open to misunderstanding; much has been written about him, and some of his interpreters appear to have less sense, less sense of reality and less sense of humour than the poet. His poetic personality and picturesque appearance are by now almost legendary yet, so Joseph Hone tells us, it was said by a banker about Yeats that he would have made an eminent lawyer and by a lawyer that he would have made an admirable banker, a finely-edged tribute to a many-sided character in danger of becoming a victim to his own legend.

Yeats's life as a young poet was troubled and hard, but unlike Sturge Moore, who might have led his life almost at any stage in history and who would perhaps have been most at home in Renaissance Italy, Yeats was a man of his times and success came comparatively soon to him. Public events were influenced in their course by him because his character and extra-literary activities, as well as his poetry, touched the imagination and affected the deeds of his contemporaries: and conversely he was as a poet changed and developed by the happenings around him. The revival of Celtic lore, Madame Blavatsky's adventures in spiritualism, the Irish nationalist ambitions, political and literary, the Irish troubles and beautiful revolutionary Maud Gonne, the Abbey Theatre, all contributed to his poetic experience and at the same time helped to keep him in the mind of a public who might have forgotten him had he merely been one of the great poets. It is significant that within a twelvemonth of his election to the Irish Senate he was awarded the Nobel Prize for Literature and became an international celebrity.

Sturge Moore on the contrary is little known outside a small circle of fellow poets and craftsmen, critics and friends to whom his work has always been of first importance. The facts of his life can be briefly told. His paternal grandfather, Dr. George Moore, of Plymouth, was a physician of some distinction who wrote several books including a book of verse. His father, Dr. Daniel Moore, also a physician, married first Anne Sarah Miller and second Henrietta Sturge, and had eight children: by his first wife Anne, and by his second Thomas (born 1870), Daniel Henry, Henrietta, George (the philosopher), Helen, Joseph Herbert and Sarah. Thomas's maternal grandparents, Henry and Lydia Sturge, were first cousins and belonged to the Quaker Sturges of Gloucestershire, but the Moore family were brought up as Baptists. Henry Sturge had previously married Helen Newman, and one of their daughters, Helen, married Georges Appia, a Lutheran clergyman who was also an amateur artist; their children 'first half-cousins' to the young Moores, were Cécile, Henri, Louis, Caroline, Charles and Marie, later to become Marie Sturge Moore, wife of the poet.

Thomas was educated partly at Dulwich College and partly at home. He later studied at Croydon Art School and at Lambeth

Art School, and in 1888 joined Charles Ricketts at the Vale, Chelsea, working with him and Charles Shannon and C. J. Holmes on the Vale Press productions. His literary career began in 1892, when several poems were published in *The Dial*, and covered almost fifty years, his last book of poems *The Unknown Known* appearing in 1939. He married Marie Appia in 1903; his son was born in 1905 and his daughter in 1907. In 1919 he was awarded a Civil List Pension in recognition of his distinguished service to the cause of literature and the arts. In 1944 he died.

Such are the facts. The story of his life may, it is to be hoped, come later, for he told his friend Robert Trevelyan that few novels had so good a plot, so many sudden changes and unforeseen events, and such a constantly sustained interest. At all events a study of his character and of his works, particularly the longer poems, is much needed. Meantime there are signs of a legend: Sturge Moore wrote obscure poetry on lofty themes, had Quaker ancestors, clerical relatives and a fine beard, and so was a good, humourless, neo-Victorian prophet progressing in an ordered sphere remote from the ordinary chaos of life. Nothing could be more false. In him a passion for beauty in all its forms and a mind of unusual intellectual integrity, his two prevailing characteristics, were so tempered by a robust sense of fun and a simple gentle kindness as to make him more than ordinarily human; the qualities of his greatness brought him nearer to not further from his fellow-men. Those who, like the editor of these letters, count him as a natural part of their lives are most fortunate, for the immediate presence of the poet, his grave personal beauty and dignified awkwardness of movement, his friendliness and the stimulating incandescence of his thought seem as living now as ever. The first impression of a visitor to the Sturge Moore household, either to Well Walk or to Steep, would have been one of laughter and confusion: the word 'uproar' might have suggested itself. The house was full of beautiful things and lively people: pictures crowded the walls, books overflowed the bookcases, and ideas and jokes crowded the minds and overflowed in the talk of the poet, his wife and children and the friends they gathered round them for poetry reading, for discussion or for less serious occasions. On one never-to-be-forgotten evening the poet and his wife paid their first visit to a cinema. It was a country cinema showing one of Buster Keaton's early films, and it was impossible to decide which was more amusing, the film in front or the remarks at the back from the Sturge Moores, who were enchanted by the new form of entertainment.

Like Yeats, Sturge Moore was not only a poet; he had other pursuits, and it can be argued that there is in the work of such men—Byron is another example—a breadth of vision not to be found in the single-minded poets such as Wordsworth, though more should not be read into this statement than its exact meaning. Unlike Yeats, however, Sturge Moore's other interests were mainly artistic: his skill as a designer and wood engraver, and his writings as a critic of literature and an appreciator of pictures have won high recognition.

Most of Sturge Moore's poetry will be found in the four volumes of *The Collected Works* and in *The Unknown Known*. It is unfortunate that his critical writings have not yet been collected but his aesthetic beliefs are expressed in *Art and Life, Hark to These Three talk about Style*, and in *Armour for Aphrodite*. He also wrote books on Altdorfer, Correggio and Dürer. His work as a designer may be seen in his own books, and in those of Yeats, and in the Vale Press and Eragny Press productions. Perhaps one of the most beautiful examples is *Axel*, a translation by H. P. R. Finberg of Villiers de L'Isle Adam's Rosicrucian play, with a preface by Yeats and a cover and decorations by Sturge Moore.

Much of Sturge Moore's poetry is undeniably difficult; he is, as Desmond MacCarthy said, an unaccommodating poet, and his verse is often obscure, sometimes even rough. The roughness is in part wilful, the result of a schoolboyish rebellion against the common rules of speech or the common connotations of words, and is in part due to faulty diction and an unreliable ear. The obscurity is both genuine and apparent only: it arises from the poet's need to express the experience of a romantic heart and an austere intellect. Sturge Moore allows himself no unscrupulous compromise between imagination and intellectual integrity, no poetic miasma to hide the steep slopes of thought, but if the reader persist he will in the end discover in the poetry a startling clarity of vision. He is an acknowledged poet whom few have the courage to read; yet once his work is known, once the effort is made, the reward is great. Anyone looking idly through the volumes and coming upon the lines to Giacomo Leopardi

Cold was thy thought, O stricken son
Of Italy, cold as the moon

or the sonnet to Shakespeare

Whether thy loves were many or but two

or Medea's Speech

Much am I wronged and Colchis far away
I curse; for there this tortured heart first beat.
Ah, gently as the summer aspen's leaves

will recognize at once what Desmond MacCarthy called 'the flashes of an incalculable intuition' and will agree with him that they are in the presence of an authentic independent poet. In reading Sturge Moore it is, by the way, important to realize how much the visual, the descriptive, value of a word counted for him; he wished to paint rather than to sing, and though Yeats was the opposite of him in this respect they both appear to have had dutiful but stepmotherly feelings towards music as an art.

Desmond MacCarthy said that one must oneself be something of a poet to suggest the merits of Sturge Moore, and perhaps that is why the entries about him in the diaries of the Michael Fields show such insight. 'Among the flickering worldly faces his has a bit of true light always there and his own. The eyes are blank with the blankness that attracted Leonardo,' wrote Katherine Bradley; and Edith Cooper, who called him 'shy and silver-eyed' and who was herself so shy and highly-strung that it was a torment to her to hear her work even mentioned, said that 'Tommy' was 'so deep down a poet and so unpoetic for the rest' that she could read her poems to him without any strain in the doing and with profit in the result.

This combination of the poet with the unpoetic gives Sturge Moore's character its individual value, and his friends used to tell each other delightful illustrations of it, a favourite being the episode of Major Crump's crocus. The Sturge Moores were taking a wintery walk around a neighbour's garden, and the poet's wife, anxious as always to be exquisitely polite and also to make sure that nothing of beauty was missed by her husband, called out: 'Oh, look, *chéri*, look! Never before have I seen such a beautiful crocus.' 'Oh yes, *chérie*, you have. Often!' he answered, and in the laughter that followed could be heard the enjoyment they shared in each recognizing the contradictions in his own and the other's character. Mrs. Sturge Moore with her warmth and care and friendliness, her elusive elegance of dress, and the indescribable charm and glitter of her spirits, drew together many friends and created for her husband the social life he most wished for. 'I saw the silver-haired Sturge Moore' a small boy once remarked of her, as if he had noted a rare bird on its passage to the South.

The poet's flashes of caustic wit, varied surprisingly by boyish jokes, and coming down suddenly from the clouds of philosophical thought, greatly endeared him to young people. These steps from the sublime to the ridiculous encouraged them to feel that they might try the ascent in the opposite direction, especially as he told them that 'Taste is naturally *bad*' and that it only improved through exercise and effort. They were touched too by the trouble he took with their immature work and the faith he had in their capacity to grasp abstract concepts.

The course of lectures on Aesthetics given in 1924 to the older pupils at Bedales School (later elaborated into the book *Armour for Aphrodite*, and modestly referred to in these letters as 'helping Crump') caused a thrill of intellectual excitement comparable only to the appearance in the wider Cambridge sky two or three years later of Professor I. A. Richards with his theory of *Practical Criticism*, and there is some likeness as well as much dissimilarity in the aesthetic approach of the two men. The lectures were indeed exacting, and it is said that an American lady teacher here on sabbatical leave rushed from the room with the expressed intention of calling in the National Society for the Prevention of Cruelty to Children. On some of the children at least they had a great and lasting influence, and even the less serious-minded enjoyed themselves analysing the aesthetic emotions of Mrs. Green who kept the village sweet shop and collected china ornaments.

It is typical of Sturge Moore, a much loved and laughed at figure, that he wrote to Robert Trevelyan after his first public speech, delivered to the Masquers in July 1903, that it 'made people laugh, but whether at me or at what I said I cannot feel sure.' Yet if by chance he had found himself, like his brother, a Cambridge professor, he would have had a distinguished success. Only chance, however, could have placed him in a public position, for combined with qualities that would have assured his success were qualities of an opposing nature that prevented him seeking it. His strong honesty of purpose made him extremely modest, self-doubting at times. He was also obstinate, and a great controversialist; in literary polemics he could be delightfully but fatally tactless and direct. More important, he was too absorbed in his work and in the life of ideas, and too generous, to spend time on practical politics of any sort.

The letters given here will be read with interest for scenes of a period rapidly growing remote, for literary judgement and prophecy, for the light thrown on the working methods of two poets and the way in which Yeats combined Sturge Moore's skill as a designer and craftsman with his own mystical ideas, for the evident generosity of both men, poor as they were, in money matters, for an irresistible and informal glimpse of the two great men licking labels to see how well they stuck, and perhaps particularly for the characters and thoughts of the two friends as shown in the long philosophical controversy. This started in December 1925 when Yeats visited the Sturge Moores at Steep and lectured on his own poetry to Bedales School. He wrote to Sturge Moore afterwards of a vision he had seen in London on his way home to Ireland. Soon Ruskin's cat made its questionable appearance in the correspondence, its disappearance, reported by Frank Harris, being even more questionable. The ensuing discussion lasted five or six years. Both men were frank and intense in the search for truth, yet they managed to maintain intellectual detachment so that Sturge Moore could say 'You are certainly wrong about my philosophy and I suspect you of being equally wrong about your own' without Yeats being more than mildly indignant: 'No, I never compared your brother to Herbert Spencer nor did I accuse him of an adulterous commerce with physical science.'

Philosophers may be tempted to explain in verse the shortcomings of the two poets in philosophical speculation. Of the two Sturge Moore had the greater philosophic bent, and he could not help laughing occasionally at his friend's unscientific ways. The editor of these letters remembers a time when Yeats was in Steep with Sturge Moore, who called looking as if he had news of importance. 'Yeats has finished his philosophy' he said (and it is impossible to forget how handsome and how serious he looked in the summer sun and shadow of the room), but more was to come, '. . . all but the central thought. He has forgotten *that*,' and a well-known wicked and amusing expression came over the face of the poet. Yeats, like other mystics, sometimes fell into the temptation of seeking to establish his beliefs by the science he wished to discredit, but no one can help being disarmed by such preludes to evidence as 'When the housemaid . . .' and 'Some German told Ezra . . .', while 'I was told so with some emphasis at Oxford' certainly dispenses with any necessity for proof. Nevertheless Sturge Moore believed that Yeats was essentially scientific in spirit, with a desire to be convinced intellectually of the truth of mysticism that was never fulfilled, so that although he was always stirred in his imagination by the paraphernalia of mysticism, and strongly attracted by the attendant thrill of conspiracy, yet he remained at heart a sceptic.

Some letters have been lost: all that were preserved have been included in this volume with the exception of a few short notes of little interest. A few cuts, made to avoid giving pain or offence, are indicated in the text. The spelling and punctuation of both poets have been corrected and small words obviously left out in haste restored without indication. In some instances it has been considered necessary to put footnotes to the letters; for the rest, a star against the letter-number indicates that notes will be found at the end in an appendix under the same number as the letter. Detailed particulars are given of Sturge Moore's publications, since they are not conveniently available elsewhere,[1] but not of Yeats's as they may be found in Mr. Allan Wade's Bibliography published by Rupert Hart-Davis in 1951. Most of the letters were undated, and some wrongly dated, and Yeats's handwriting is almost illegible,[2] so that the task of putting the correspondence into order has not been easy: it has sometimes seemed that the two poets were simultaneously communicating each in a different year—a notion of time and space that would have appealed to Yeats. Great care has been taken but the editor hardly

---

[1] Mr. Frederick L. Gwynn's *Sturge Moore and the Life of Art* (University of Kansas Press 1951, published in London in 1952 by The Richards Press) is of interest in showing that Sturge Moore's poetry is now studied in the United States, and the part of the book that records the facts of the poet's life and the chronology of his works contains much useful information though it is not accurate in all respects.

Another sign of the widening recognition of Sturge Moore was the unveiling by Lord Horder on 26th October 1952 of a stone tablet put up on the house at Steep in memory of the poet who lived there from 1919 to 1927.

[2] A few of his letters were dictated to Mrs. Yeats and a few typewritten.

dares to hope that the present order and dating are wholly correct.

The editor wishes to thank Mrs. Sturge Moore and Mrs. Yeats for their great generosity in allowing the letters to be printed, and to express special gratitude to Mrs. Yeats and Mr. Allan Wade for much kind help, to Professor George Moore, O.M., for his care in reading the manuscript and to Lord Russell for his magnanimity. The editor is also most grateful for advice and assistance given by Mr. Dan Sturge Moore, Miss Riette Sturge Moore, Miss Sybil Pye, and Mr. Lennox Robinson. Acknowledgments are due for information taken from *W. B. Yeats 1865-1939* by Joseph Hone, *W. B. Yeats, Man and Poet* by Norman Jeffares, and *Ireland's Abbey Theatre* by Lennox Robinson, and from Mr. Allan Wade's invaluable *Bibliography of Yeats*. Acknowledgments are also due to Messrs. Macmillan and Co. Ltd. for their kind permission to reproduce Sturge Moore's designs for *Reveries, Responsibilities, The Wild Swans at Coole, Per Amica Silentia Lunae, The Tower* and *The Winding Stair*, and to The Richards Press for permission to quote *A Queen's Song* by James Elroy Flecker.

THE LETTERS

Coole Park, Gort, Co. Galway.

11 August [*1901*]

My dear Moore,

Now that I have your play in print I think even better of it than I did when you read it. I am much more satisfied with your verse and your theories of verse than I was. You certainly get vivid effects out of your modern words and I do not now find any of the verse too intricate in its thought, though I do sometimes regret an inverted phrase. The play should act admirably and one regrets, vivid as they are, the few little things that do not come within the limits of the stage. If they were not there you would have an admirable chance of being pirated in America at once. They have just pirated my *Land of Heart's Desire* and played it with great success, to judge by the press cuttings, through all the chief towns. They did it with *In a Balcony* by Browning and seem to have had very much more than a *succès d'estime*. Quite ordinary papers were enthusiastic and wrote under such headings as 'The Triumph of the Literary Drama.' In Chicago at any rate they played not only to a full house but to increased prices.

All seems to me to show that if one writes actable little plays now, without too many characters, they will find their way on

A   I

to some stage. I think you have done the best play of the kind there is. I hope you will soon publish your *Herod* also.

I am starting a little heroical play about Cuchullin and am curious to see how my recent practical experience of the stage will affect my work. I have a strong plot, with some ironical humour. The play is part of a greater scheme. I am doing all the chief stories of the first heroic age in Ireland in a series of poems. I have just finished a half narrative half lyrical poem of about 200 lines which I think good.

Theseus himself is I think about the finest, but all the characterisation in your play is good—perhaps 'the maidens' do not seem of very 'good family' but they are all the more vivid.

Yours sincerely

W. B. YEATS

2*

18 Woburn Buildings, Euston Road, London.

Saturday [before 21st Oct. 1901]

Dear Sturge Moore,

Yes, I shall come with pleasure on Wednesday 9th. You do not say what hour. I shall assume that it is seven unless you write to the contrary.

Excuse my delay in answering but I have had an influenza attack and have had other exciting episodes.

Benson's company accept for Irish production the legendary play I have done with Moore, and Mrs. Pat Campbell accepts for London. Business matters, amount of royalties etc., have yet to be settled. I see the acting-manager on Monday to settle detail about Mrs. Pat Campbell's production.

The play is prose so that it should find none of the difficulties ours had to meet.

Yours sincerely

W. B. YEATS

3

18 Woburn Buildings, Euston Road, London.

Dear Sturge Moore,   *Tuesday [before 21st Oct. 1901]*

I am sorry to say that I am so full of rheumatism and neuralgia that I shall have to disappoint you tomorrow. I should have written before but I thought to be well by this. Yesterday however—the result of a walk home from a friend on Sunday I think—I developed bad neuralgic headache, and today after waking quite well I have found it come on again though less severely. I am very sorry. I have had to write to Benson, who had sent me a box, to postpone that too until next week. I had hoped to go to his theatre on Thursday. He is I think taking over provincial rights in *Grania*.

I hope you will let me dine with you as soon as I am well. This weather has upset me in a way weather has never done before, and rheumatic fever is on, the thing I have always to be steering round (for I have had it twice) and with that rock about I can spread but little sail.

Yours always sincerely

W. B. YEATS

4*

Coole Park, Gort, Co. Galway.

My dear Sturge Moore,   *[early 1903]*

I am going to ask you to undertake a rather troublesome matter. I am going to send you a bundle of plays to get copyrighted. Mrs. Emery, who would have done this for me, is away and for certain reasons these plays have to be done at once. Miss Horniman, who knows I think about stage matters, will I have no doubt help. You will be able to do the whole thing in an afternoon. The plays after they have been sent to the Censor will have to be gabbled through on a properly licensed stage—

say the Victoria Hall. Two people must know their parts but the smallest parts will do. There must be a bill outside—the smallest —and one person must pay for admission. Money handed back afterwards. Your little company will just have a reading on a stage instead of at your rooms. You will have to pay something for the hall—I got one for ten shillings last time—and for printing a bill.

Will you send the plays to the Censor, or, if not, will you send me his address? It might be as well for you to send them. I will of course send you a cheque for the cost. The Censor will have to get £1 an act (the worthless creature). I can send you the plays in all likelihood next week. I am sorry to give you this trouble but if I did not I should probably have to go to London myself as these plays must be licensed at once. On second thoughts you will have to send the plays to the Censor as you will have to tell him the date of performance.

Miss Horniman's address is 1H Montague Mansions, Portman Square. I am sure she will get you any information you cannot get.

Yours always

W. B. YEATS

I shall be very glad of your criticism of the plays.

5*

[Early 1903]

Dear Yeats,

I have done the best I could for you. It was no use attempting a coloured sketch as I had neither the colours of the dresses nor of the background. I think a raw undyed material would be best for the walls and ceiling. If it is not hung on the blind principle it might be stretched on canvas stretchers but this would be more expensive. The floor should be coloured with the stuff they use to reddle sheep with, which is very cheap. Mrs. Morton, the housekeeper at 20 Fitzroy Street, could tell you where to get it in case Fay did not know. She uses it for doing in behind the stoves. The angel ought not to wear wings or she could not get through the door, and no one must lean against the walls etc.

There is no need for doors, which are expensive if workable, and as long as there are doorways all that is needed is there.

Hoping this will be in time and answer its purpose.

Yours sincerely

T. S. MOORE

The master's desk is to stand bang in the centre of the stage but near the back wall, leaving only room for his stool behind it.

6*

Coole Park, Gort, Co. Galway.

[after March 1903]

My dear Moore,

I don't like the colour scheme at all. I know the effect of gauze very well and it will not pull this scheme together. The white sail will throw the hounds into such distinctness that they will become an irritation. I found that the brown back of a chair during the performance of *The Hour-Glass* annoyed me beyond words. Further, the black, brown and white effect is just one of those effects which we like in London because we have begun to grow weary with the more obvious and beautiful effects. But it is precisely those obvious and beautiful effects that we want here. The fault is very largely mine, for you had, as you thought, to bring in the red, black and white hounds. Now that I have had to think things out I have come to the conclusion that the hounds must be all in some one colour and be almost lost in the main colour of the sail. Your scheme would upset all my criticism here. I have been explaining on these principles:—

1. A background which does not insist on itself and which is so homogeneous in colour that it is always a good background to an actor wherever he stand. Your background is the contrary of all this.

2. Two predominant colours in remote fanciful plays. One

colour predominant in actors, one in backcloth. This principle for the present at any rate until we have got our people to understand simplicity. *The Hour-Glass* as you remember was staged in this way and it delighted everybody.

Now what do you mean by backcloth to be continued? The wings of a theatre are ordinarily about this proportion to whole stage.

If we continue your bulwark or sail in a straight line a man at A will see into the machinery. If we arrange our stage with enormous wings we will not fit into some of the halls we may have to play in.

We shall have to bring the scene round like this

I have been working this out on a model and it has been a rather troublesome thing. The sail had better slope like this when seen from front, as that will hide the view into wings best and enable sailors at end to fight half hidden by the sail as they are meant to.

I have written to Fay for the exact measure of his stage, which is now a little larger than it used to be, the size of wings, etc.

Now as to colour scheme. The play is dreamy and dim and the colours should be the same—(say) a blue-green sail against an indigo-blue backcloth, and the mast and bulwark indigo blue. The persons in blue and green with some copper ornaments. By making one colour predominate only slightly in backcloth and one only slightly in persons the whole will be kept dim and mysterious, like the waters themselves. What do you think?

Now as to costumes. Nothing later than [*illegible*]th century, Wagner's period more or less, though a more modern touch no harm. We want to keep to a vague period that our costumes may be combined and re-combined in various plays.

Have I worried you too much over the thing? I can carry it out myself but I would far sooner that you did. If you were over here five minutes' conversation would put all right and you could work as many hours a day as you like with your Shakespeare.

If I have not disgusted you and put you out of patience I can send you the exact measurements after I have got all right on my model and in consultation with Fay.

I hope all goes well at the meeting on Saturday. I have written a letter to be read out. Nothing yet from Gilbert Murray. I had not got his address so wrote care of Lord Carlisle.

Yours ever

W. B. YEATS

7

7*

Coole Park, Gort, Co. Galway.

My dear Sturge Moore,

May 6th [1906]

Many thanks for the name of Appia's book which I have asked Miss Horniman to get. I tried to join in that controversy but nothing worth having would come though I wrote a lot.

My people are setting out on the first regular professional engagement at the ordinary theatres. Tree's manager has engaged them for an English tour—they will I think however take nothing but peasant work.

I am sorry you have chosen *Salomé*, though *The Florentine Tragedy* will probably make all the difference between success and failure as it will bring the old audience. I think the Wilde audience is limited to a few hundred who have already been; but my real objection is that *Salomé* is thoroughly bad. The general construction is all right, is even powerful, but the dialogue is empty, sluggish and pretentious. It has nothing of drama of any kind, never working to any climax but always ending as it begun. A good play goes like this

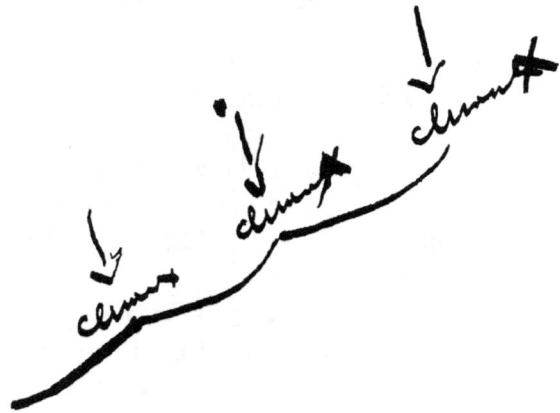

but *Salomé* is as level as a table. Wilde was not a poet but a wit and critic and could not endure his limitations. He thought he was writing beautifully when he had collected beautiful things and thrown them together in a heap. He never made anything organic while he was trying to be a poet. You will never create an audience with any liking for anything by playing his poetical works. No good actor will ever succeed in inorganic work and you will get yourself into the hands of the amateurs and the dilettante and of vulgar charlatans like Farquharson.[1]

I have nearly as strong objections to the Hell act out of Shaw's play, though different ones. That too has no real dramatic life. To do anything you must have a group of players who will stick to you and learn the business of simplicity and imagine that your present 'people' will by this get a chance, and you must write and choose such plays as will display them at their best, never on any excuse of expediency or convenience putting upon the stage inorganic work which means boredom for them and therefore bad work for them and boredom for all.

Yours ever

W. B. YEATS

P.S. It is not in the least because of anything I say or think about *Salomé* but I wish you could put somebody else on that Committee in my stead. I have made a general rule of confining work to Ireland for the present and also of never making myself nominally responsible when I cannot give the time to work at a thing properly. My Irish work gets every day more exacting.

[1] The Literary Theatre Society gave performances of these plays on June 10th and 18th 1906 at the King's Hall, Covent Garden. *Salomé*, with Miss Darragh in the title rôle, Robert Farquharson (Robert de la Condamine) as Herod, Florence Farr as Herodias and Lewis Casson as Jokanaan, caused a scandal on account of the Biblical subject. Charles Ricketts, who designed the costumes and setting for both plays, and who was already at that time a dramatic critic of wide experience, told 'Michael Field' that Robert Farquharson's Herod was one of the greatest pieces of male acting he had ever seen.

9

8*

[*after October 1906*]

My dear Yeats,

I must write to thank you for your *Poems* which has given me far more pleasure than any of your other books. *The folly of being comforted* and *Never give all the heart* are the best of their kind ever written and I am deeply in love with *Baile and Aillinn*. The tone of voice is perfect and the rhythm and rhymes exquisitely suited to it. I could only make one tiny criticism, that is I wish you could invent something a little more worthy than your 'orchard' to come before your 'glass boat' on page 160. I think 'fruit of precious stone' and 'apples of the sun and moon' the most loathsome upholstery that was ever invented to cushion poetry with and would prefer plain wood. But those four lines are the only ones in the poem which are not intoxicating.

Baile's Strand is greatly improved though I still think there are a few weak places. I like it very much. *The Shadowy Waters* is improved also but I can't say I believe in it wholly even yet. And *The King's Threshold* is now I think as good as could be though I should like the hanging at the end to proceed a little further before the king was converted, and think it would be more effective if there was a scene in which the hanging was proceeding and the king kept saying 'your pupils will be swinging in a moment' and sending out to ask if they were yet strung up and only at the last moment when Seanchan had said to the king 'You will be hated for ever for this' the king should relent and the pupils be sent for [and] reprieved.

Yours sincerely

T. S. MOORE

9*

20 St. James's Square, Holland Park, London.

14 September 1907

My dear Yeats,

I must write to tell you how much I have enjoyed your *Deirdre*. It is very beautiful and very original; the verse in its very texture is quite an invention of your own, and the construction admirable, though I think the mood one of the most difficult to present dramatically. How I should like to see it adequately rendered! I think it would produce the effect of a religious mystery by the perfection of its seclusion from the world and the rare distinction of its self-decreed limitations.

> *'I never heard a death so out of reach*
> *Of common hearts'*

is exquisite.

> *'There's no body like him, for he forgave*
> *Deirdre and Naisi'*

has a most pathetic and yet dainty effect, and

> *'I'd not have you believe I'd long stay living'*

and

> *'The very moment these eyes fell on him*
> *I told him' etc.*

That is a new simplicity and a most enchanting one that you have found in these lines which give the key and tone to the finest speeches:

> *'That I go look upon him that was once' etc.*

perfect!

But the most perfect is the atmosphere of the whole and the way it is all of one fineness, I think far beyond anything I have ever read of Maeterlinck's and in a similar kind of excellence.

11

I still prefer *Baile's Strand* because of the subject which is in itself greater, but I quite understand that you will feel this to be more subtly complete. Perhaps I also feel that some of the verse in this, because the new rhythm is so assuredly found, begins at times to hint at a monotony which has come from the time of it having grown an obsession and obtruding where another less original would have given relief.

Of course the Song *Love is an immoderate thing* is one of your very best. You have made your new note perfectly pure and clear and it delights me far more than the most sounding rhetoric run in the old moulds can do even when it is most simple.

I hope next time you come to London we may be in a position to invite you to spend the evening with us, but owing to servant worries and domestic events we have had to deny ourselves the pleasure of being hospitable for a long time.

Yours ever most sincerely

T. S. MOORE

10*

Nassau Hotel, Dublin.

4th October 1907

My dear Sturge Moore,

It was a great pleasure to get your so appreciative letter. I often get rather discouraged about my playwriting, at least so far as the verse is concerned. The little plays I have written in prose are ever popular here, but it is so difficult to get good performances of verse work, and good audiences for it, that one rather loses heart. There are a little group of enthusiasts here who care for it, but they are only a small number in comparison with those who like prose comedy, and then the critics generally tell one that one should go back to the lyric.

A man has just sent me from Australia, with an evident belief that I would like it, an article which he has written commending that damned *Innisfree* and repeating phrases out of every article telling me I know nothing about drama written by a person called Shore, I think, in *The Academy*. I find that people have no sense of dramatic Art as an Art, but only of the nature of one's subject. You are dramatic if your subject is easily understood and sympathised with by the average man, and you are undramatic no matter how carefully you construct if you look for a special audience. We shall do nothing till we have created a criticism which will insist upon the dramatic poet's right to educate his audience as a musical composer does his. I hope you are not giving up dramatic writing. Miss Horniman whom you know has a theatre now at Manchester which is producing verse work, and her manager Payne is quite an intelligent man.

I really like *Attila* though I could see that Binyon was not easy because of having to construct for the first time. The first result of construction when one works at it deliberately is to make one rhetorical. There are such a lot of things that have to be said not because one wants to say them but because the plot insists on them. I think it is only when one has so mastered construction that one is conscious of nothing but the subject that one is able to think of so arranging the story that one need never go beyond oneself.

Please remember me to Mrs. Sturge Moore.

We produced a crude comedy by a new man three days ago, and it is, it seems, going to be a great success though it represents the people in a worse light than Synge ever did. They object to Synge because he is profound, distinguished, individual. They hate the presence of a mind that is superior to their own, and so invent and even believe the cry of immorality and slander. But it is much the same everywhere; nothing is ever persecuted but the intellect, and the one thing Plutarch thought one should never complain of is the people. They are what they are, and it is our work to live our lives in their despite. Where they are crude as here they are perhaps less mischievous than where they believe themselves educated and read *The Spectator* or write it.

I have done a tragic farce—I know not what I call it—with Lady Gregory, three acts, and will produce it this winter.

Yours ever

W. B. YEATS

I I

20 St. James's Square, Holland Park, London.

11 October 1907

My dear Yeats,

Many thanks for your letter. I am sorry you are so discouraged and hope you may get a real chance before long. Think of Shaw's position before the Court started and Shaw's position now. Most people would have said that the more part of his plays were even more hopelessly unfit for the public than verse plays. That may give us hope.

What you say echoes a passage I had been translating for an article from Baudelaire's journal. 'Nations produce great men only against their will—as families do. They strive all they can not to produce them. And thus the great man in order to exist must needs possess a force of attack greater than the power of resistance developed by millions of individuals.' There is truth in that but it is not all: events favour good work and great men sometimes, and the current of events is always veering. If the great man persists suddenly he will find it with him when he least expects it, often when he no longer deserves it. If we persevere in deserving it we shall be able to profit by it when it comes; to find it come and no longer to be able to profit by it would be hell indeed.

Did you mean to suggest that I should do well to send a play to Miss Horniman? And, if so, ought I to address it to her or to Payne? And what address for either of them?

Attila will very probably be given in Berlin; it is not certain yet. A Russian who is here was quite disgusted by the way the verse was delivered; in Russia it seems verse is always spoken as verse and prose as prose! Wonderful country!!

Even the most intelligent people like Ricketts, Shaw and Barker don't believe that possible because they can't imagine it.

Please remember me very kindly to Lady Gregory.

Yours ever

T. S. MOORE

12*

Coole Park, Gort, Co. Galway.

May 1st [1909]

My dear Sturge Moore,

Your letter has been sent on to me here. I have just I hope finished a revision of the second act. I must wait a day or two until I can dictate the new scene to Lady Gregory's typing. I will then send you the play. It would be great luck if Mrs. Campbell would play it at the Stage Society. I thank you for your good offices in the matter.

My revisions are to make the second act richer in speech, more like Act I.

You might ask the Stage Society not to read Mrs. Campbell's version of the play but to wait for my improved one. I have retouched the heroine's part a little but chiefly worked on Septimus.

Yours ever

W. B. YEATS

13*

Fairfield, Glasnevin, Dublin.

February 9th 1910

Dear Sturge Moore,

I want you to do a small thing for me. I am to give a series of three lectures in London in March at a private house; one lecture is to be on contemporary poetry and the last half will be a eulogy upon your work. It is very important to me to be able to give a preliminary lecture on the subject to get my thoughts into shape, for I cannot prepare for a lecture on paper beyond a certain point. My only chance is next Sunday evening. I wrote to the young man to whom I have lent my rooms to send me all of your books that he can find; he did so but he did not send me what I want. Can you send me the little brown paper-covered book containing a poem called *Kindness* and also *The Vinedresser and Other Poems*. I will take great care of these volumes and let you have them back without fail. If I get the lecture right I shall certainly deliver it in a number of places, possibly in America. I am sorry to trouble you. I am taking you as the typical poet of the movement immediately after that of The Rhymers' Club.

Yours ever

W. B. YEATS

Please send the books the moment you get this or they will not be in time.

14

18 Woburn Buildings, Euston Road, London.

Saturday [21 January 1911]

Dear Sturge Moore,[1]

I have got a marked copy of the *Review* from the office and will see Harrison on Monday. I have had correspondence with

[1] This letter and the next refer to the publication in January 1911 by *The English Review* of Sturge Moore's short story entitled *A Platonic Marriage* and headed by a remark from Dr. Johnson's *Preface to Shakespeare*:—'The writers of barbarous romances invigorated the reader by a giant and a dwarf.'

The story is a period piece, none the worse for a Wildean tinge in the dialogue, and is interesting to the student of Sturge Moore's style and development as a writer, particularly in relation to *Hark to These Three talk about*

Gosse on the subject but as he marks his letter confidential I can only say that I think you need not be anxious. The Home Office is quite reasonable on matters of this kind. I find also that Harrison's manager is not really anxious. I think Harrison has perhaps tried to make your flesh creep and is perhaps happy in the thought of his heroic attitude. I wish for your sake and that of The Academic Committee they would send him to prison. I would not spare him a sigh. The longer he was there the more use he would be.

Yours ever

W. B. YEATS

15

18 Woburn Buildings, Euston Road, London.

Tuesday [*24 January 1911*]

Dear Moore,

Gosse has seen the Home Secretary (this is confidential) who is friendly and will do nothing, but if the Vigilance people move on their own account they cannot be stopped. But I think nothing will be done. I had a long talk with Harrison on Monday on the telephone. I don't think he will go to prison—it is a pity. The Academic Committee cannot move officially but individual members would help in case of a fight.

Yours ever

W. B. YEATS

Style published in 1915 (Elkin Mathews). The pitfalls of the theme are avoided rather ingeniously; and there are some striking passages of intuitive reflection, as well as one or two characteristic awkwardnesses. Robert Trevelyan and the author both liked the story though the Vigilance Society were able to view it as indecent and made an attempt to get the January 1911 issue of the *Review* suppressed. The editor, Austen Harrison, was prepared to suffer in the cause of literature but no martyr was needed as the affair never came to anything.

16*

c/o Lady Gregory, Burrin, Co. Clare.

Saturday [4th April 1911]

My dear Sturge Moore,

Last Tuesday you were elected a member of The Academic Committee of English Letters. Several names had been proposed and then I proposed yours, upon which the proposers of the other men withdrew their men and you were chosen unanimously. There is still a formality to be gone through. Our vote has to be ratified by the Council of the Royal Literary Society of which we are a part and this is why your name has not yet been put in the press. The two names put in *The Times*, Benson and Hewlett, had been virtually elected at a previous meeting and their election ratified but there had been some technical error. We had therefore to accept them with the other work of the provisonal committee. You are however one of the thirty original members. The secretary will let you know the date of the next meeting and also tell you when your name has passed the Royal Literary Society.

I think we may do a great deal with the Committee to uphold unpopular excellence.

Yours ever

W. B. YEATS

17

16 Rue de Fleurus, Paris VI.

25 April [1911]

Dear Sturge Moore,

I believe we are to have a meeting of The Academic Committee on May 11th though I have not yet had formal notice. A tendency is arising to nominate for an election only safe men, and this is being caused partly by the fear of getting men rejected and so giving them rather a shock. The present idea of the members who were present at the last meeting of the General Purposes Committee of five (I was not present) is to propose Belloc and Doughty. I am strongly for Belloc and I think suggested him, and not so much for what he has done as for what he is. He is French enough to know about Academies and I think will support a bold course of action. There is no need to make any effort about him. If proposed he will be elected. Doughty I know nothing of; he may be a very good man, but if elected it will be because a man so little known is quite safe. Are you for the election of Shaw? I think we should have him, though I think his work arises out of a fundamentally wrong principle and won't last. Even at that it is better than the work of some of the people we have and what we want is vigour. When a man is so outrageously in the wrong as Shaw he is indispensable, if it were for no other purpose than to fight people like Hewlett, who corrupt the truth by believing in it.

We need three people to nominate anybody, at least I think that is our rule. You and I and, say, Binyon can put up Shaw. He may not be elected but we must risk it. Even more important, for I think it would be easy to get three people for Shaw, is will you join in nominating Wilfrid Blunt? I would ask George Wyndham, a great friend of his, to propose him. Only a small part of his work is good but that is exceedingly fine, and he also is vigorous. I am thinking a little of your own recent adventure in wanting people of this kind. With a little more support in the Council we can get the idea of an authoritative pronouncement on the relation of literature to such prosecutions. A thing of the kind would make us an Academy at once. We had some discussion on the General Purposes Committee. I found little opposition but not enough earnest support from any quarter to make it desirable to press it at the moment. I think they are gradually coming round to it.

Would you mind answering my two questions by return of post.

Yours ever

W. B. YEATS

18

20 St. James's Square, Holland Park, London.

26 April 1911

Dear Yeats,[1]

I had always understood that Chesterton and Belloc were the two buttocks of one bum. Now I learn that you are as strongly for the one as against the other?!! I doubt whether Belloc has any French instincts left, certainly no academical ones. I shall vote against him.

Doughty wrote an epic in eight volumes, not English but a concrete of all the jargons spoken since before Chaucer. The volumes are upstairs so I know. When young he wrote a book of travels in a kind of riotous boyishness somewhere between Richard Burton's and Furnival's. This had a certain felicity of its own but he is old now, old, old! I shall vote against him.

I am strongly for Shaw. He is the only known genius among living writers, the others are all *méconnus*.

I am not against Blunt; he is a horse dealer, a calling which should foster insight.

Barker is a man of far truer intellect than Belloc, not that I want him elected. He is one of those painfully honest people who

---

[1] In 1939 Sturge Moore wrote to Joseph Hone that he was 'dumbfounded reading my old letters. I had totally forgotten that I had been so violently opposed to Belloc, and at first could not conceive the reason but by degrees I came to the conclusion that it must have been because he mixed Catholic political propaganda with literature, one of the major crimes in my early judgement. . . . I rejoice that I was so definitely for Shaw and E. M. Forster. . . .' He was most anxious not to pain Mr. Belloc, who had shown him much kindness when they came to know each other later, and he did not wish to offend Granville Barker, for whom he had much respect. To avoid making public criticism he no longer felt to be just, he directed that this letter should be cut if published, but the cuts and omission marks he indicated gave a misleading impression, and so it has been agreed that the letter should be given in full with this explanation.

in time to come might defend a journalist who had dubbed a Butcher '*great*' by giving that adjective a significance it never had before.

Why elect anyone but Shaw?

However I am willing to join in nominating Blunt, if need be.

A pronouncement about prosecutions for immorality and indecency is no doubt desirable provided they have the courage to make it definite. But have they?

I don't believe in acting on principles: the only ones I believe in condemn us all equally and so give no one any right to take the offensive in defence of them. This is *à propos* of Shaw's work, much of which I detest, but that does not alter his merits.

Yours ever

T. S. MOORE

P.S. I think young Forster should be nominated; he at least has always tried for literature and nothing but literature. Each one of his novels has been better worth reading. He is clean. He is young. We shall very likely show foresight in electing him. I would much rather vote for him than Blunt. E. M. Forster, who wrote *Howard's End*, *A Room with a View*, *Where Angels Fear to Tread*. He has quite a following and of the right sort. I have no doubt Binyon and Newbolt would be willing to nominate him.

Why go for people hopelessly prostituted in politics and journalism when one could have a man like that! It is insane! Belloc? No! a thousand times no! It is disgusting. You read *A Room with a View* and see what you think.

19*

Coole Park, Gort, Co. Galway.

28 July [*1911*]

My dear Sturge Moore,

I think 'purity of language' means merely [to] uphold style as opposed to slipshod popular writing. A writer's 'purity' is his

21

truth to his own mood. Balfour was asked but refused on the ground that he was withdrawing from everything but politics and Shaw was not asked because the Society of Authors Committee, which advised as to names, advised against him on the grounds that he was such a trouble on a committee. The Academy will be what we can do with it and this is a matter of courage. Very sorry you have been ill.

Yours ever

W. B. YEATS

20*

Coole Park, Gort, Co. Galway.

Sunday [*1912*]

My dear Sturge Moore,

No, I am sorry but I prefer my own versions. I have made one change; for 'sky' in *The Source* is either a misprint or something put in by   *   *   *   *   *   I brought both versions to Lady Gregory and told her I did not know which was yours and which mine. She said both (the poem was *The Source*) were bad, though 'buds of enchantment' less good than 'poppy buds,' but 'coyly open' impossible, and finally said the version in print was the best. She was emphatic against the changes in *On the sea shore* but in that case she knew they were not my changes. I took a great deal of trouble with these poems and used the words 'buds of enchantment' which I dislike because the flowers in Bengali are connected with an Indian fairy tale which is the association Tagore wanted. I do not want to alter anything now when I have forgotten the reasons I had when working over these poems. I have left one change, that on page 19.

Yours ever

W. B. YEATS

P.S. On going over *The Source* I have made a slight change and put in 'poppy'.

22

Sturge Moore's design for the cover of *Reveries*

21*

Stone Cottage, Coleman's Hatch, Sussex.

26 January [*1916*]

Dear Sturge Moore,

Emery Walker writes to me that he will be sending the block to America in a few days. Have you given him the directions about the binding, the thinness of the canvas back etc. that they may go with it?

I see that you have had the sort of press that one always gets for poetical drama. It is not business, and so the critics can express the irritation which they have long felt against all plays whatsoever, without injuring the advertisements in their papers. I wish I had had a chance of criticising, but if I had I would have been so savage about the performance that neither Barker nor his wife nor the man who stage-managed, whoever he was, would have ever forgiven me. I am convinced that if I had the play in my hands, and if I was free to cut one long passage after the death of Holofernes, I could have made it grip all the part of an audience which cares for literature of any sort. It is a logically expounded situation, varied and unified. It just wants to have those things taken out which as a matter of course are taken out of practically every prose play in rehearsal. The moment one goes into rehearsal one discovers, among other things, that the stage picture is so much more powerful than the words that there are whole passages which lose their weight. A shifting of the centre of gravity takes place and this involves minor changes. Then, I would secure for you that the words would be heard, and, what is even more important, that they should be attended to. *That woman* thought of nothing but herself and her poses, and her poses were as disagreeable as herself. She never lost an opportunity of facing the audience, nor of tossing her arms about. She exhausted every possible movement of her body in the first five minutes, and when she came to her important scene she had squandered her whole capital and yours with it. She showed herself throughout with neither brains nor heart and even had she achieved what she wanted to it would have been a cinematograph show suggesting bad Academy pictures. I have seen her poses in the past good but I realise now that they were good because they were arranged by Barker.[1]

Let me know if you can come and dine with me next Monday. Could you let me have a postcard addressed here?

Yours ever

W. B. YEATS

22*

c/o Madame Gonne, Colleville, par Vierville, Calvados.

August [*1916*]

My dear Sturge Moore,

I have just asked Macmillans in London to send to Macmillans in America a complete set of proofs of *Responsibilities*. So the moment has come for the cover. Have you arranged with Watt about it? (A. P. Watt, Hastings House, Norfolk Street, Strand).

I am starting Iseult on what I hope will grow to be a book about the new French Catholic poets. What do you think of Péguy (whom we are reading), Claudel, Jammes? Which is the most admirable? Péguy I find impressive but monotonous. His Jeanne d'Arc dialogues are I suppose the first dramatic or half-dramatic study of a saint which has reality but I cannot judge his style.

---

[1] *Judith*, by T. Sturge Moore, was acted on January 23rd, 1916, at the Queen's Theatre by the Stage Society, with Lillah McCarthy as Judith. That Sturge Moore disagreed entirely with Yeats's criticism is shown by his dedicating the play, when it appeared in renovated form in volume II of his *Collected Works*, to 'Lillah McCarthy, now Lady Keeble, the splendid actress and beautiful woman, whose genius revealed, with its virtues, the faults of my play.'

I have written a great mass of my *Memoirs* which will be published only after my death—at least as a whole.

Yours ever

W. B. YEATS

Did that money reach you?

23

c/o Madame Gonne, Colleville, par Vierville, Calvados.

24 August [1916]

My dear Sturge Moore,

Will you be in London next week, when I hope to get back? If so write to Woburn Buildings.

About Péguy. I am impressed by the completeness and self-consistency of his vision of the events of the Incarnation and by his resources in expounding all appropriate feelings as they arise. At the same time I am well aware that if Fiona Macleod wrote in a foreign language and somebody read it to me I would over-rate the work. I would not see the looseness and redundance but put all such defects down to the imperfection of translation. I admit that Péguy does not speak to me personally as Jammes does or as Claudel does, and that I am always dramatising myself as a pious woman in a country village and saying 'Ah, how that would affect me!' Jammes asks of us often a similar condescension but then he is not quite serious. I hear that the earlier books of Péguy are very bad. His Christianity is of course for us impossible—how take all simply when the very authority of texts is in question? Read the opening of the second volume of the *Joan of Arc*, the long bit about the woodcutter. It has matter, a little over-stated at moments, but full of invention, but has it style? Fiona Macleod also had matter but only very occasional style. If Fiona had style throughout the best of the stories would have been masterpieces. When I say Péguy's Christianity is impossible I do not mean that he is insincere.

Yours always

W. B. YEATS

Sturge Moore's design for the cover of *Responsibilities*

24*

c/o Madame Gonne, Colleville, par Vierville, Calvados.

[*summer 1917*]

My dear Sturge Moore,

I send you £14.13.10 to settle account. I also send you back the book cover. I think it excellent. I suggest that you do it all in the same thin lines, rose and all. This is merely a suggestion—have thick lines for the rose if you will. I have a notion that the rose will look more luminous in the same thin lines as the rest; it is itself a convention that one knows and yet so simple that it could hardly be changed. I think it a fine grave design. I am telling Watt that you will write to him direct about it. A. P. Watt & Son, Hastings House, Norfolk Street, Strand.

I am living in a house with three and thirty singing birds, which for the most part have the doors of their cages open so that they alight on the table during meals and peck the fruit from the dishes. There is also a Persian cat, a parrot, two dogs, two rabbits and two guinea-pigs and a Javanese cock which perches on Madame Gonne's chair.

Yours ever

W. B. YEATS

When my sister sends back the needlework to you I will get you to arrange with Mr. Old to put it on the wardrobe.

25*

Ballinamantane, Gort, Co. Galway.

[*before 28 July 1918*]

Dear Sturge Moore,

I have been making enquiries and I am convinced that a child's cot cover would be a very valuable thing for my sister. People

Sturge Moore's design for the cover of *Per Amica Silentia Lunae*

are not using table centres now. Would you mind allowing my sister to use your Infinite Fold for a cot cover? It would be a delight to a child or any child's mother, being a most lovely thing. And besides I know that my sister can get a commission for it at once. If my sister got the material for the table centre we shall find means for using that later. The table centre might be used for exhibition purposes later. Now about the material. You would want a thicker material, possibly a thick Roman satin. How is your sight? Have you yet got your glasses? Don't make any adaptations of the Infinite Fold. It is perfect as it is.

Yours ever

W. B. YEATS

26*

40 Well Walk, Hampstead, London.

[*before 28 July 1918*]

My dear Yeats,

I think the idea of applying the Infinite Fold design to a child's cot coverlet a very good one. But I do not think it a reasonable idea that I should let your sister do what she likes with my design. I have taken the trouble to find out where silks and wools can still be obtained and am furnished with cards, and I shall expect her to order the numbers I quote from the firms in question. Or, if she likes to send me samples of all the materials and colours she has by her I will use them as my palette and adapt the design to them. But I cannot consent to the design being carried out with only a vague and varying reference to the colours I chose. I think I can now work on it right away and she can have it before the end of August right enough, but she must let me know the measurements of the coverlet and send samples of materials or agree to use those I have discovered. I think it might be worked on an Irish linen, white or unbleached. I have got my glasses now and the block is in hand.

I have not yet been called up and the Doctor who examined

30

and rejected me for the French Red Cross two years ago says I am almost certainly grade III and am practically certain not to be called out.

I have been very busy with all kinds of jobs lately but shall now settle down to the Fold and the block. How are you getting on? Are you in the castle yet? How are you working and on what? I suppose you are having a soak of rain just as we are. Remember me kindly to your wife.

Yours ever

T. STURGE MOORE

P.S. Your sister wrote, June 12th, 'it is not a bit of use colouring by the shade-card. I will carry out your ideas as closely as I can; every day it becomes more difficult to get colours.' That is why I suggest that she should send samples of materials she actually has. The cards I have are nearly a year old now though I have no doubt I could obtain anything obtainable through the Headmaster of Leicester School.

27

Ballinamantane, Gort, Co. Galway.

28 July 1918

Dear Sturge Moore,

I did not for a moment mean that my sister should choose her own colours, but merely that you should not redraw or recolour a design already suited to the purpose. No change in the proportions for instance is necessary. I rather think however that I did say that the material you showed us would be unsuitable for this purpose. I don't like the idea of an Irish linen, white or unbleached. The particular purchaser I have in mind wants a rich colour and unshiny surface. Would you like me to ask her to send patterns? If the design is to be much used, as I hope, I am afraid you must accept the fact that the material worked on will have to vary according to the taste of the purchaser, as it will have to fit into different schemes of decorations. I will ask my sister to send you the size. It might be the best way to work for you to let the purchaser see the design as a guide to the choice of material. I am afraid you won't like this idea but I believe it to be an essential of the market. The design will of course be always the same in colour and form. In work of this kind one is always making a part, not a whole. The whole is the room. The present purchaser wants for instance a dark colour, whereas some-body living in an Adam room would want your white Irish linen perhaps. One thing certain is that a woman whose friend has your design on emerald green, let us say, will insist on having hers in purple or sky-blue—horrible as it may sound. The present purchaser is not in a hurry, as she would prefer to wait a little in order to get a fine piece of stuff. The moral therefore is, send the design and let her see it. It is quite right in proportions. My sister can magnify it without changing the proportions.

Send my sister the cards, marking thereon the silks you want, and ask her to send you samples of the nearest she can get.

Don't put off the block for anything. We are impatient, partly because we think of taking a suggestion from it for a lantern of stained glass to hang in our hall in the Castle.

Yours ever

W. B. YEATS

28

40 Well Walk, Hampstead, London.

[*after 28 July 1918*]

My dear Yeats,

I am afraid it is no good and some other design had better be used. My design is not suitable for working on any ground chosen by any idiot. Its principal colour is bright green and so the blue and purple loving ladies will not want it. Your sister proposed cherry-cream or blue in a note I received from her by the same post. So evidently we are all talking at cross-purposes. I am willing to design with any colours so long as there is a fair range of choice and could adapt the motive of the Infinite Fold. But the actual design done cannot be swapped about from one colour to another to suit what somebody may imagine to harmonise with her bedroom. If your sister sends me an envelope full of snips of colours she actually has and a few patterns of simple grounds that she can get I will go to work. But it is madness to talk of grounds of purple and blue for the actual design and shows a complete misconception of the nature of the problems involved. How could my colours be kept in such a case? I am quite willing to do a new design when I know what the stable conditions are. Until then I get on with the block.

Yours ever

T. S. MOORE

29

73 St. Stephen's Green, Dublin.

17 November [*1918*]

My dear Sturge Moore,

We have both a great admiration for the bookplate. Get it printed by anyone you think fittest—Emery Walker or another as you please. I wonder if you could do a cover design for my new book of poems *The Wild Swans at Coole* but Macmillan say they will only give three guineas. What did you get before? The book contains all my recent poems, the Mabel Beardsley poems and so on. I wonder if the *Per Amica* design with a new emblem would do—a torch, a candle in waves, a hawk, a phoenix, a moon, a butterfly, a hunchback.

The purchaser for the cot cover is ourselves as we like very much your design that you showed us at Oxford exactly as it was then, in colour and all (especially in colour) but my sister cannot begin till after Christmas. She will send you patterns of silk. She has a very large range of colours.

We are in a great hurry for prints of bookplate. I think it is one of your best works. I enclose cheque!

Yours ever

W. B. YEATS

Cover design wanted at once. I have already revised first proofs.

30*

(Postcard)

Postmarked Holmbury St. Mary.

4th January 1919

I see I have been writing to you at No. 73 St. Stephen's Green and you are really at No. 76. I am well on with the two covers and think of a mask in a circle with a rosary for *The Cutting of the Agate*. I have written to Macmillans and received a dummy book etc. I have heard no more of your sister nor have I received any wools and silks from her, so the cot design is hung up. Are you going to let the Stage Society do your *Player Queen* at once? Can't you get Mrs. Pat to act for them? That would be the best arrangement.

Yours in haste

T. S. MOORE

31*

The Shiffolds, Holmbury St. Mary, Dorking.

My dear Yeats,   [*February 1919*]

    I have received an early copy of *The Wild Swans at Coole*, and hope before they send you one they will put right a mistake which originated on my drawing—'of Coole' instead of 'at Coole.' The design is much less well printed than that for *Per Amica* was and I have also remonstrated about that.

    I have much enjoyed reading your poems, many of which are new. The Elegy on Robert Gregory is I think one of your very

34

Bookplate for Mrs. Yeats by Sturge Moore

best things. Reading it again I liked it even better than at first, and there are quite a number of others which I rank very high and am glad to have to hand so that I can improve my acquaintance with them.

Someone has suggested to me that you are thinking of the quilt for a real baby and that that is why you are stopping in Dublin this winter. The idea had never entered my head as you spoke so decidedly while at Oxford in a contrary sense. But I hope the event has been brought to a happy termination and that both mother and child are doing well. We are anxious to learn whether the world is enriched with a boy or a girl,

I have sent in the design for *The Cutting of the Agate*, which is a further development of the scheme of this new cover, and I think is handsomer though it will probably not please so many people.

Have you seen anything of the fight between me and MacColl in *The Times Literary Supplement*? So far I seem to have had decidedly the best of it. I never dreamt of rousing him when I began.

Yours ever

T. STURGE MOORE

32*

4 Broad Street, Oxford.

15 March [1921]

My dear Sturge Moore,

I want you to do a design for the next Cuala book—*Four Years: 1887-1891*—a new autobiographical work of mine; something like your candle in waves. Would a hawk do? Your hawk on the cover of *Responsibilities* is such a fine beast. I use the hawk as a symbol once or twice in the book. The hawk could be perched or flying, or perched and hooded. Perhaps I may think of something else or perhaps you may.

Yours ever

W. B. YEATS

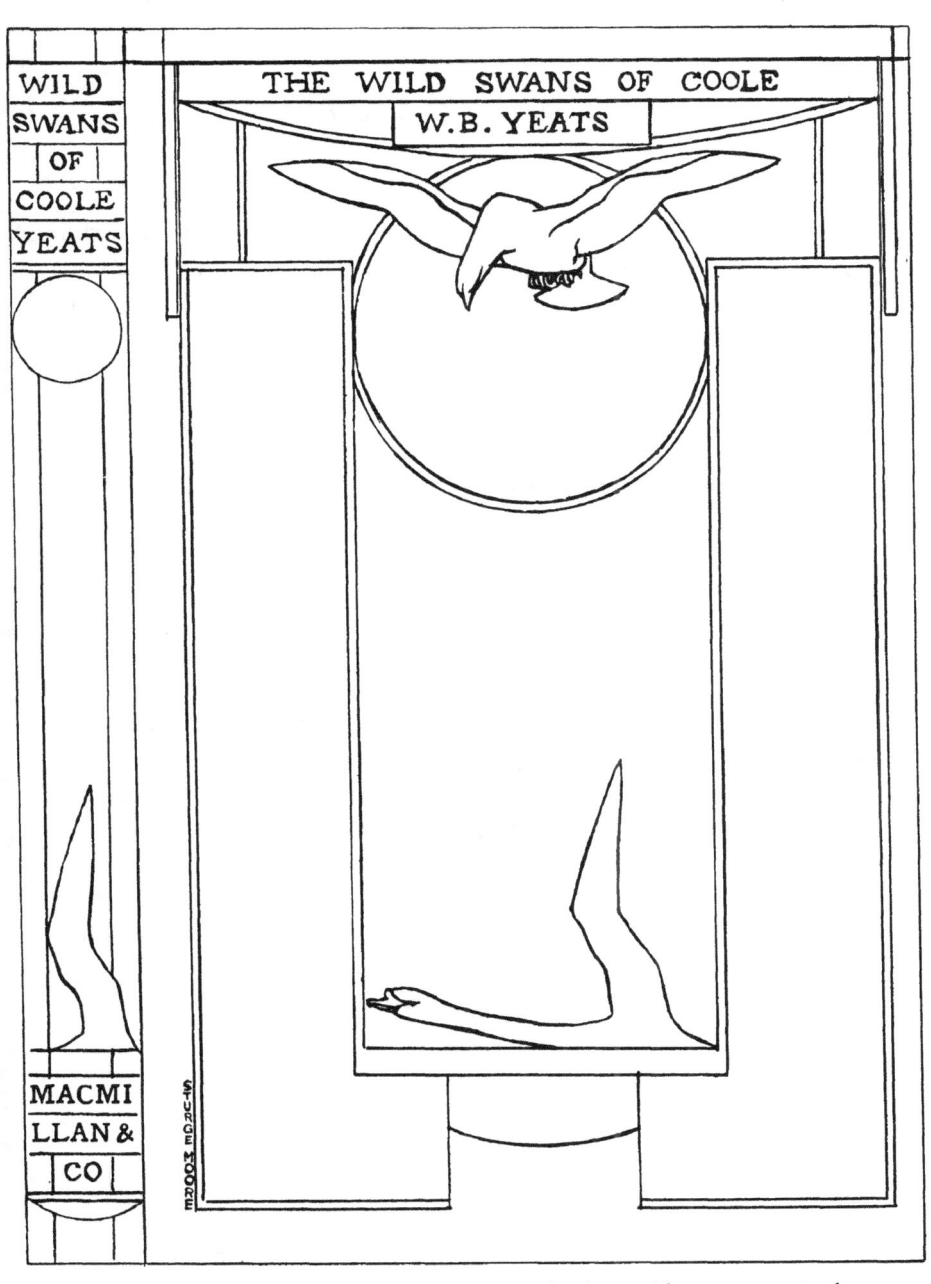

Sturge Moore's design for the cover of *The Wild Swans at Coole*

33*

Cuttlebrook House, Thame, Oxon.

Private

6 September [*1921*]

My dear Moore,

I am sorry for it would make a fine design but don't nail the hawk on the board. The hawk is one of my symbols and you might rather crudely upset the subconsciousness. It might mean nightmare or something of the kind for some of us here. Life when one does my kind of work is rather strange. I wish I could suggest something but nothing occurs to me. My main symbols are Sun and Moon (in all phases), Tower, Mask, Tree (Tree with Mask hanging on the trunk), Well.

Yours ever

W. B. YEATS

34*

Hillcroft, Steep, Petersfield, Hampshire.

[*after 6 September 1921*]

My dear Yeats,

Perhaps you have seen or will soon see my cover. I shall be very anxious to hear how you like it. They have reproduced it very well and I think it is very effective. I had done a more elaborate design which had its good points but I feel this is most practically successful. Please don't worry about the crucified hawk, which was rather a pictorial than a decorative idea and went with the other rejected features.

I like your plays a great deal, and especially some of the poetry in the Emer play:—

'*A woman's beauty is like a white*' etc.

and

'*Who is it stands before me there*'

which I think are up to your high water mark. The play I like

Bookplate for Yeats by Sturge Moore

least is *The Calvary*. The other three I think each successful in its own way, though *The Hawk's Well* most so. Surely some action of Emer's, not the mere thought of her but a visible intervention, ought to have defeated the Woman of the Sidhe. But I like the play greatly all the same.

We hear that you are to be congratulated on the birth of a son and send our best wishes and congratulations both to you and Mrs. Yeats.

T. STURGE MOORE

35
4 Broad Street, Oxford.

7 November [1921]

My dear Sturge Moore,

I send this to Macmillan to forward as I am in Scotland lecturing and have not brought your address. I am delighted with your cover for *Four Plays*—it is particularly admirable as a black and white design. Hawk a little less good than the rest but that is probably my fault for objecting to your crucified hawk. The design is however one of the best you have done, taken as a whole

I have just read Hall Caine's *Rossetti*, and as I read Rossetti's letter; was constantly reminded of Ricketts. He must when very young have formed himself on Rossetti. I cannot define the resemblance but I am sure of it. There is the same apparent lack of philosophy with the same occasional philosophic insight and there is the same occasional over-generosity of praise, but there is something beyond all that which I cannot get at. This book of Hall Caine's does give something of the man which the big life published by Bell, which I have, does not. In what books should one look for Rossetti as a thinker about literature? Where does one get his letters? I have an impression that there is no real life though much scattered material. Am I right? What a life to write! But I suppose questions as to who bought this or that picture would always crush the interest out. I wish you would write it or put the doing of it into some picturesque head. One wonders if the personal part is somewhere in private letters that may not be published for many years. By the way I heard a detailed story of Mrs. Rossetti's suicide. In any work I have looked at it is set down as accidental death. I have also heard a number of supernatural stories.

Yours always

W. B. YEATS

36*

[8 November 1921]

Dear Yeats,

Many thanks for your note. At present I am plunged in books about Leonardo da Vinci as I hope to write a poem about him. When I have done I will reconsider your Rossetti notion but I doubt if I am quite the right person. I will let you know when I next come to London, as I should like to come on to Oxford and see you again if it was convenient. The enclosed is my first effort in engraving with a knife on the plank.

Yours ever

T. S. MOORE

37

Hillcroft, Steep, Petersfield, Hampshire.

8 November 1921

My dear Yeats,

I was glad to get your letter and learn that you liked the design. The earlier one was in some ways better, much richer and more complicated, and I was afraid they would not print it well enough but they have done this one so much better than ever Grant Richards has got one done that I think I could have trusted it to them after all had I known how well they could do such things when well paid by a firm like Macmillan's.

As to Ricketts and Rossetti, I think there are great resemblances as you say, derived from their Italian blood, but I am still more conscious of the differences. I knew Ricketts before he became so entirely absorbed in Rossetti as at one period (about 1890 or 1891) he was, and I cannot say that I think he modelled himself consciously on Rossetti at all. Very early there began to be criticism of Rossetti's personal life. He was 'a lousy beast.' His undignified happy-go-lucky personal address offended Ricketts. As an artist I doubt if he influenced Ricketts much more than Gustave Moreau did or Puvis de Chavannes, etc., etc., though I think that there was something in Rossetti's best things that was more closely felt by Ricketts even than Gustave Moreau's best. Still it was G. Moreau he wrote about in *The Dial* and not Rossetti, though I think he ranks Rossetti far higher now. Ricketts certainly did many first-rate designs entirely founded on Rossetti but so he did on G. Moreau and Burne-Jones even.

We lived at that time in an atmosphere of anecdotes and appreciations of Rossetti. But, as I say, though delighted by these anecdotes and laughing over them, Ricketts also greatly disapproved of the unbuttoned Rossetti. He greatly admired poems of Rossetti which I have never cared for, because they seem to me heavily artificial or rhetorical, such as *Love's Nocturn, The Stream's Secret,* and *Cloud Confines,* but he put before all these *The Portrait* and *The Blessed Damozel,* in which I was entirely at one with him, just as we agreed over which were the finest sonnets, though he also liked secondary sonnets like *Willowwood* more than I did.

About narrative and dramatic poems, *Sister Helen, The King's Tragedy, Troy Town, Eden Bower,* we were quite at one in liking them though I am less enthusiastic now. It may have been as a reaction, to avoid Rossetti's mistakes, that Ricketts began to be more careful of his person, but of course this also coincided with rather more money making such care fruitful, and meeting more people, but there was also something 'stuffy' in Rossetti's mind which he disliked, 'something of the period and milieu' he would say.

We read in those days Hall Caine's *Rossetti* but perhaps you are referring to a recent book by him which I saw reviewed in *The Times* but have not read. W. Michael Rossetti published several volumes of letters; besides these were Madox Brown's *Life*, W. Bell Scott's *Memoirs* and Holman Hunt's *Recollections*, but a good deal came to us by Herbert Horne and Gleeson White who gathered it from all sorts of artists and others who had known him. May Morris later on added some stories. I should say that, could he be bothered, Ricketts could write an ideal Life of Rossetti, or at any rate an extremely interesting one. He remembers better than I do such stories and he has such extremely illuminating comments to make on the pictures and poems. *Soothsay* and *The Burden of Nineveh* are the two most philosophical poems by Rossetti and we admired both a good deal, but I think Ricketts then thought that Rossetti's mind and genius were more perfectly expressed in some of *The House of Life* sonnets like *Known in Vain, Inclusiveness* etc., etc.

Fanny, his mistress, model, cook and housekeeper, the original of *Lady Lileth* and the *Lady with the Fan*, was something of a medium and afterwards married the keeper of a small public house in Chelsea and gave *séances*, to some of which I believe Horne had been. It is only the photo of *Lady Lileth* before he repainted it that reflects or idealises her features; he afterwards made her quite different and not so interesting. He kept his money in a drawer to which Fanny had as free access as himself, —one of the reasons that made it necessary for Watts-Dunton to come and live with him, as Fanny abused her privileges and was as lazy as Rossetti.

Rossetti certainly dabbled in spiritualistic experiences at that time but the only definite story I know or remember is the one given by Bell Scott about his conviction that a certain Chaffinch was his wife's soul. Watts-Dunton promptly persuaded him that he was an Agnostic, though at bottom he was a very Christian mystic. But this belongs to the drug-taking period when his painting was going to pieces, though some of his best sonnets belong to it. I don't imagine from what I vaguely remember that Fanny in later life was at all a good medium, but at that time I paid no attention to such things but scouted the whole subject as superstitious nonsense. I never heard what Horne said from himself but only from Ricketts and Shannon in the mornings after they had learned such things overnight, as I always went home and did not sleep in the Vale but only worked there. They also regarded spiritualism as mere rot. So what I might have learned in that subject was allowed to slip and never lodged in my mind. Perhaps Hueffer would know something about it? Burne-Jones's Life[1] is very interesting and casts some light on Rossetti but not a great deal, chiefly on the Red Lion Square and Oxford periods. The references to the later Rossetti are extremely discreet. I always understood that though there was a good deal of presumption that she might have committed suicide it was also quite possible that, maddened by neuralgia, she took an overdose of opium by accident, which of course was the version conventionally agreed on. But I think there could be no proof either way. Only, Rossetti had not been treating her altogether well and the circumstances of their life were sufficiently squalid and unsuitable to the recovery of an invalid who may very well have felt them to be hopeless. Apparently he had given her reason to be jealous, as well as neglecting her and leaving her very much too often alone for long hours.

But I expect you will think there is far too much of this scribble. I do not think that details about who bought what pictures need interfere in writing it as one could send the reader to Marillier's *Life* and the corrections of fact that his information needs could

[1] Probably *Memorials of Edward Burne-Jones* by Lady Burne-Jones.

be given succinctly in an appendix. Why don't you write it? Ricketts would no doubt help.

Yours ever

T. S. MOORE

P.S. Of course one of the chief sources of stories about Rossetti was Oscar Wilde though where he got them from or how much he edited them I cannot tell. Also later Fairfax Murray. Of course Wilde probably had had some from Ruskin.

38

4 Broad Street, Oxford.

24 November 1921

My dear Sturge Moore,

Forgive me for dictating this to my wife but I have got into such arrears of my letters that I shall never be through them unless I use artificial light which involves dictation. I will try and write later on.

I am greatly obliged for your most important letter about Rossetti which I shall carefully preserve. I shall never write a biography of anyone for I have not the patience for objective narrative. I think you should do it, and that if *you* do not no one ever will who has any chance of recording any of the floating stories. Of course somebody will do it some day from the published material alone. It is however an immense opportunity, and an opportunity for speaking out about a whole generation, and should have a very great success.

I have been sent copies of the American edition of my *Four Plays* and I notice that they have used your cover design. I am delighted, but I had nothing to do with the matter and if they have not paid you they should be made to do so.

If you are up in London any time after Christmas extend your journey a little and come and stay with us.

Yours ever

W. B. YEATS

39

Thoor Ballylee, Gort, Co. Galway.

15 August [1922]

My dear Sturge Moore,

Werner Laurie may ask you to look through the final proofs of my *Trembling of the Veil* but this will only be if civil war prevents my doing so. He will send me proofs and I will return them at once but if they are lost in the post or greatly delayed he will send a set to you. I shall be sorry to give you this trouble but all is uncertain here. Last night I heard two explosions at 4 a.m. and now there are no trains for the two bridges have been blown up. Letters I think will go as the mail cart carries them to Galway. All the time I do not spend on proofs I spend on a series of poems about this Tower and on the civil war at which I look (so remote one is here from all political excitement) as if it were some phenomenon of nature.

Yours sincerely

W. B. YEATS

Lady Gregory's and Edward Martyn's are the only large houses within many miles that have not been raided and one great house has been burnt. The casualties are however slight. One hears of some man killed and then nobody for many days. A motor has just passed with a National soldier and a coffin up on end and what I suppose were the relatives of the dead man. Owing to the blocking of roads this bye-road has become a main thoroughfare. That may be ended by the blowing up of our bridge. The National army is in control here and the people are with them but the Irregulars come out at night. I wonder how the future of European civilisation will be affected by the rejection of majority rule, first in Russia and now in Ireland. It may lead to a Military Government or at any rate to a powerfully armed Civil Government.

40

Hillcroft, Steep, Petersfield, Hampshire.

My dear Yeats,   *20 August 1922*

I was very glad to get your letter as I have often thought of you anxiously, though consoling myself that if anything serious happened to you it would doubtless find its way into the papers. I shall be very pleased to look through your proofs for you, should that prove to be necessary, but I think we may hope that things will soon begin to be better and communications be re-established. It seems likely that the De Valera party are on their last legs and can hardly hold out another week, so by then the worst will be passed, though it will take long to get everything into working order once more.

We are just off to Paris for a month. My address will be c/o Mme. G. Appia, 9 rue Val de Grace, Paris V. The proofs would be sent on to me or you could let Werner Laurie have my address when you next write. I will drop them a card in case you should not be able to do this.

Hoping that Ireland's troubles are nearly over and that they will not be followed by similar ones here or in France.

Yours ever

T. S. MOORE

I hope Mrs. Yeats and the little ones are well and happy in spite of explosions etc.

41*

82 Merrion Square S. Dublin.

My dear Sturge Moore,   *17 July [1923]*

I fear there is no chance of my getting over for July 21st. But it is exciting news, and I shall be most anxious to see your mask. Have you any photographs of it? I am deep in a new Nōh Play myself. I am held here by politics and some other matters.

I am very anxious to have a talk with you about the big design for the philosophy book. I have now written about 120 pages and these pages are being typed. If I can arrange with Macmillan for Laurie to take the book we could have several designs of various kinds. I think the big main design must have a Unicorn in the middle. Perhaps when I get over next—and this may be in two or three weeks; it depends on Lane picture politics in part—I may run down to see you.

Life is amusing here. I had a guard till a week ago who opened the door automatic in hand, and I have two bullet holes in my windows. However, the return of quiet is a great relief to the nerves.

Yours sincerely

W. B. YEATS

42

82 Merrion Square S. Dublin.

18 August [*1923*]

Dear Sturge Moore,

I return herewith the 2/6 in the form of a postal order. I should have sent it before but had first a most crowded week in Dublin, and then Ballylee and a cold, followed by a return to Dublin, and after that more Ballylee. So cold, business and trains must be my excuse.

I am at Ballylee but get back to Dublin by August 24th. Little harm has been done here, despite rumours in the press, and even in the neighbouring towns, except the windows and doors burst in and various traces of occupation by Irregulars, stray bullets, signs that a bed has been slept in and so on. The Irregulars took care of our property and even moved a Russian icon of my wife's from a dry wall to a dry shelf, but after they had gone the country people stole all the mirrors. They left the blankets and such humdrum property but evidently found a novelty not to be resisted in the large mirrors. The same has happened elsewhere, men even stealing mirrors that would not fit into the thatched houses and had to be left outside to be charged by enraged cows.

48

I find that Dulac has actually begun designs for my philosophy, or rather practically finished a portrait of Giraldus as frontispiece. He offered some time ago but I had not taken him seriously as I know how busy he is. He says he wants to do also the big diagram to keep the two in harmony. If he does so I shall ask you to do something else for me instead. I have asked The Macmillan Company to get certain covers from you and if they consent this will be an occasion to press for payment of their old account. I have also another job in my head.

Have you heard that as a result of my sister's illness my wife has taken charge of the Cuala embroidery and that the whole industry is moving into 82 Merrion Square? My wife is full of energy of mind and body and will I think greatly improve the work. She knows what people wear and has seen modern art. My sister's work had become too sere[?], a ghost of long past colours and forms. I look forward to living in a house where there is so much going on.

Perhaps some day you will come over and see us. Dublin is talking well, and if war does not break out again in the winter, as is very possible, will be a pleasant place to live in.

I shall always have a very vivid memory of your masked demon. He had a consciously religious effect, but very old Greek religion, suggesting some return of forest and shrine. I wish you would write such a ritual and let us join the worship. Your garden city would be easily converted.

Yours ever

W. B. YEATS

43*

82 Merrion Square S. Dublin.

1 November [*1923*]

Dear Sturge Moore,

I have put off from day after day writing to you because of my sight. Your *Judas* is in small print and I am passing through one of those periods when my eyes smart at strong light or small print or much reading of any kind. I have got however through enough of your *Judas* to see how vivid it is, especially in that ghostly Cities part, where I have read some long passages. Lady Gregory read it all while here and was impressed by it. I wish I could work on your great scale instead of cutting my seal rings.

Nothing settled about covers with American Macmillan yet. They are objecting to boards. I may have to accept plain labelled buckram to escape their impossible cloth though I know their buckram will be almost as bad as the cloth.

Since my sister's illness my wife has taken charge of the Cuala embroideries and is making a success. They needed a new and younger eye.

Yours ever

W. B. YEATS

44

Hillcroft, Steep, Petersfield, Hampshire.

7 November 1923

Dear Yeats,

I was very pleased to have your letter but very sorry to learn that your eyes are troubling you again and hope that they may soon recover once more. I am glad you like so much of my *Judas* as you have been able to read. We have not been able to make out quite all the words in your letter. I think in many ways that shorter poems are a better thing to produce than long ones, quite apart from the fact that they have a wider public. So few people can give the time and patience necessary to become really acquainted with a long poem. And, though they perhaps give that to only one in ten or twelve of the short pieces of the poet they prefer, he at least becomes more definite for them than the author of a poem they only tried to read and meant to return to but didn't.

I never feel really like writing poetry now until I have worked up a whole atmosphere, and so I must be long for lack of power to be short.

I enclose a letter from one of the demonstrators at the School of Medicine of the London University. These young women who mean to be doctors are amazingly devoted to poetry and give up half their lunch hour once a week to read it together. They are a very sympathetic audience and if you could spare time when you are in London some time to go and read to them or talk to them they would be very delighted and count it no end of an honour. They are quite simple and unpretentious and far more enthusiastic than critical. You will see that De La Mare has been, and I went.

I am glad to hear that Mrs. Yeats is waking up the Cuala Industries, and hope you are all well.

Yours ever

T. S. MOORE

P.S. Could you just let me have a p.c. to say if there is any chance of your being able to accede to their request, and when, so that I can let our friend know.

45

82 Merrion Square S. Dublin.

23 November [*1923*]

Dear Sturge Moore,

Yes, it[1] will be a great help to me in several ways. Here especially it will help. I will find it easier to get the Government to listen to me on artistic things. I look upon it as a recognition of the Free State, and of Irish literature, and it is a very great help. People here are grateful because I have won them this recognition, and that is the distinction I want. If I thought it a tribute to my

[1] The Nobel Prize for Literature.

own capacity alone I, being a very social man, would be far less pleased.

Yours ever

W. B. YEATS

I go to Sweden on December 5th and receive the award there on December 10th. I shall spend a few days at Stockholm and Amsterdam and Antwerp to look at pictures and be back for Christmas. My wife comes with me.

46

Hillcroft, Steep, Petersfield, Hampshire.

June 1924

My dear Yeats,

I have promised to write to you. They propose to do one of your plays here next February, either *The Green Helmet* or *Baile's Strand*, and they would very much like you to be present on that occasion, and if you would consent to give them a talk about your experiences with the Abbey Theatre or any other subject you may prefer, then they would look forward to that one as the most perfect of all weekends. It will seem strange to you that they should look so far in advance, but the only way to get things of that importance done in a school like Bedales is to begin months before, as the amount of free time is very limited and the holidays make great blanks, and everything else must be decided on before actual rehearsals can begin. Besides, the committee that in future is to be responsible, instead of Mr. Badley as in the past, is new to its work and very anxious not to fail by putting things off till it is too late.

The details cannot yet be decided but the kind of programme would be a dress rehearsal on Friday evening, the performance Saturday evening and on Sunday afternoon your talk to the school. I am now helping Crump the English master, so as to help pay for my son living as a boarder in the school during his last year, and I know that you have many ardent admirers among the young people here. You might either come down here for two or for one night—we should be very happy to put you up— or for longer, and if Mrs. Yeats were able to come too we should be only the more delighted.

You will probably have heard that I underwent a rather important operation last Christmas. I am now fully re-established in health, and only a little more subject to fatigue than before, but the doctors say that will gradually wear off. Unfortunately my wife is at present in hospital having had an operation, but she is expected to recover very soon. So we have been rather in the wars since I last saw you.

Hoping that you and yours are all in good health and prospering.

Yours ever

T. STURGE MOORE

P.S. They would be very pleased to pay your expenses or to give you a modest fee, not according to your deserts but their abilities.

47

82 Merrion Square S. Dublin.

26 June 1924

Dear Sturge Moore,

When I got your letter I was saying to myself for the twentieth or thirtieth time 'I must write and ask Moore how he is.' I had heard about your illness from Ricketts and then after the operation I had heard again, so I knew that you were going on all right.

I recommend the school to do *The Green Hamlet* rather than *Baile's Strand*, at least if they think they can manage the scenery, which involves a sudden darkening of the stage. I suppose they perform to their students only and to friends, and that is to say to an invited audience, so that no question of a fee arises.

Now about my lecture. If you can really fix so far ahead with a reasonable chance of keeping to the date, I will promise to come and I will not make any charge for coming, neither a fee nor expenses, except that I will ask you to put me up while I am at Steep or get me put up. By fixing the date so long ahead I shall be able to arrange other things at the same time. I have always one or two things to do in London and it does not really matter very much upon what date I go there so long as I know it beforehand.

Could you design me, at your usual rates, a couple more ornaments for the Cuala Press. We are using the old ones again and again. If you can, I will send you a list of possible topics. I think also that my wife wants to get a bookplate for our daughter Anne; this sounds premature as Anne is not yet six, but my wife wants to have it ready for the first sign of interest in books. Are you doing such things now? and at what rate? The bookplate you did for my wife was a masterpiece and it is possible that she may want to send you some suggestions as to its subject.

Yours ever

W. B. YEATS

Baile's Strand needs too great a range of emotion for an amateur.

48

Hillcroft, Steep, Petersfield, Hampshire.

[after 26 June 1924]

Dear Yeats,

I have been expecting to hear from you about motives for the designs you said you wanted. And recently I have been meaning daily to write and let you know that your visit here is fixed for the third weekend in February next year, and *The Green Helmet* is to be the play. I hope that now you will soon write and also that you are in good health as well as your family.

We are once again all well here.

Yours ever

T. STURGE MOORE

49*

82 Merrion Square S. Dublin.

21 October 1924

Dear Sturge Moore,

I was yesterday told by my doctor that I must abandon all public work for the present. After a speech in the Senate the strain produced considerable pain. I am suffering from high blood pressure and have to avoid every kind of excitement. I am afraid I have no choice therefore but to abandon my journey to you in February. I have had to give up all lectures and have been advised to go to another country and climate as soon as my philosophy is finished. I am trying to get a secretary in order to finish this book and calculate that in three months I shall be in Italy. I am putting aside every other work so that I may be able to work at this book without too much strain and am asking my wife to look after my letters.

I shall try however, before I abandon them, to send you directions about that bookplate. I am sorry to disappoint you and your friends in the matter of the lecture, and if I can get my health reasonably normal again will deliver it later. My life has been too exciting it seems and I must now pay for it. A book with me has been like a drinking bout, or at any rate the doctor seems to think so, having questioned me in vain for more normal excess.

I hope you are all well again. I saw something of Ricketts when I was in London, and something of his castle.

Yours ever

W. B. YEATS

50*

Hillcroft, Steep, Petersfield, Hampshire.

[after 21 October 1924]

My dear Yeats,

I am exceedingly concerned to hear of your seizure. Would it not be better to finish the philosophy in the South and so get the benefit of a sunny winter right away? After such a summer as we have had everybody needs sun, and you more especially with this attack behind you.

Everybody is very sorry to learn that your lecture must be postponed.

I shall hope to receive instructions for the bookplate. I have had a great deal of trouble over *Axel*, fighting hard for every inch of beauty against both publisher and printer, but I begin to think I shall win through in spite of the prospectus, which was odious and for which I was not responsible, and in spite of the great difficulty of getting things done through somebody else who himself does not understand where you are driving. If I do, it will be a fine book.

Hoping to hear that you have decided for Sicily or Algeria before the cold sets in, and for Italy in the spring.

Yours ever

T. S. MOORE

51*

82 Merrion Square S. Dublin.

28 October [1925]

My dear Sturge Moore,

Do you remember that lecture that I promised you and could not give because I was ill? I have to be in London on the 30th of November and will stay on for a week or so, and I could give the lecture if either Wednesday or Thursday December 2nd or 3rd would suit you, and if you would still like the lecture. I have still only the two subjects I think I mentioned to you; first, the Irish Dramatic Movement and second, My Own Poetry which is much the better lecture of the two. I am always hoping that I may find a third or fourth subject, and may now that my big book is finished and my thoughts free. Let me know if you would like me to come down as I must fix up my week. I am not giving any other lectures but there are certain friends I want to see.

Yours ever

W. B. YEATS

52

Hillcroft, Steep, Petersfield, Hampshire.

1 November 1925

My dear Yeats,

I was very glad to see your handwriting on the envelope yesterday. Mr. Badley the headmaster says he will be delighted and that either the second or the third of December will suit perfectly. They would like the lecture on your poetry best. They will not be able to produce *The Green Helmet* for that date as the Christmas Shakespeare play will be in rehearsal but will hope to do it later on when perhaps it may be possible for you to come again. I am glad to learn authoritatively that your health is again good and that your big book is finished.

We will expect you on Wednesday 2nd of December unless we hear that you prefer the Thursday (in which case please write) and I hope you will let us put you up at least for that night.

Hoping that Mrs. Yeats and the children are well.

Yours sincerely

T. S. MOORE

53

82 Merrion Square S. Dublin.

12 November 1925

Dear Sturge Moore,

You will forgive my dictating this to my wife but I have had a very busy day going through schools in the morning and the Senate in the afternoon. We have a new Education Bill coming on here and I have a speech to make on the subject at the Irish Literary Society in London, and all the usual political intrigues to manage here. And by the way I shall want to pick up some information at Bedales if I can: no, not Bedales; you will be able to tell me all I want to know.

I will come by the early train, the 10.15 from Waterloo, that I may have some talk with you and that I may get a rest in the afternoon. I am quite well now but I have the habit of lying down in the afternoon as I get tired easily. (I shall come on Wednesday as you suggest and lecture that night.)

It is very kind of you to put me up and I am looking forward very much to seeing you. May I stay the Thursday night too? George thanks you very much for asking her too but she has been away lately and can't get away so soon.

Yours ever

W. B. YEATS

54*

82 Merrion Square S. Dublin.

8 December [1925]

My dear Sturge Moore,

It was very pleasant to see you and your wife and all that good company you gathered for me. I thank you.

Please do not let the school send me any fee. I was wool-gathering when you spoke to me about it. I proposed myself as lecturer and cannot possibly accept anything.

The night of the day I left you I made an old friend see a vision. For about a minute she sat turning the pages of a missal invisible to me and describing the pictures. Hitherto I have always taken the idealist view of such visions but now, thanks to your brother's *Refutation of Idealism*, I am permitted to think they exist outside the human mind. I wish however that the missal, now that I must think it of the same stuff as the table, had lasted longer for it was a handsome book. Part of the vision I shared or rather produced by my unspoken thought so we had a common element. However that is really irrelevant to your brother's, though not to Bertrand Russell's, argument. I am deep in his *ABC of Relativity* but incline to reverse the argument and see light as stationary—the divine mind is one of its aspects—and all visible things revolving within at so many hundred thousand miles a second. It is almost the argument of *Siris*. They revolve and yet are also stationary—Time in its double nature and in one of those absolutes.

Yours sincerely

W. B. YEATS

55

Hillcroft, Steep, Petersfield, Hampshire.

14 December 1925

My dear Yeats,

I was very glad to learn that you were safely back at home and were deep in Russell on Einstein. I have, alas! not yet turned to Gentile. I very much hope you will not return the honorarium to cover expenses which I gather has been posted to you from Bedales. For the sake of others you should accept it or they begin to think that it does not matter what they accept without return.

I do not think my brother would consider his arguments properly used to deny the possibility of hallucinations. Because some appearances have real external causes does not mean that

59

others may [not] be entirely subjective. Memory may be as vivid and precise as the experience remembered. He only furnishes reasons for supposing that the universe does exist independently of the consciousnesses aware of it, not that those consciousnesses may not be subject to hallucinations, bad logic and other diseases.

Like common sense and medical science he considers this distinction extremely important.

Russell's *The Problems of Philosophy*, in the Home University Library, gives an extremely lucid and brief summary of the main arguments. It is a cheap 2/- book published by Williams and Norgate.

With best wishes to yourself and Mrs. Yeats (I sometimes see visions of possible dancers for Anne's bookplate—one on a tiny island dancing between the moon and its reflection in a lake. Would that mean anything propitious to you?) and thanking you again for your friendly and most enjoyable visit,

Yours ever

T. S. MOORE

P.S. I went to the International and saw Dulac's *Adam and Eve*, the most important thing he has yet done. I feel that the tone of the flesh is too isolated in the composition and should have been balanced by other pale colours elsewhere. But Adam's attitude and expression are very happy and the plants and birds and squirrel beautifully done. Many thanks for your Catalogue.

56

82 Merrion Square S. Dublin.

5 January [1926]

My dear Sturge,

I am delighted with that Chapter IV of *Problems of Philosophy* in which Russell puts his and your brother's argument. If we have 'an act of apprehension,' a 'sensation,' we must not infer as Berkeley did that the object apprehended is in the mind. This error has, Russell says, entirely made idealism 'of no validity whatever.' *If an act of apprehension, a sensation (say) of colour or of weight, could be proved to exist without an object it would obviously refute Russell's argument. I am therefore right in finding in this Chapter IV proof that my friend's dream missal really exists.*

I once saw a seer lift a dream stone from the ground with obvious sense of its weight. That stone too exists. Thank God; it is such a simplification. And to think that the only possible disproof of its existence is a mere confusion of thought caused by substituting the word 'idea' for 'sense-data.'

The rest of the book grows out of this chapter and all applies to those dream-objects which a number of people share by telepathic communion. But for that first argument one might be contented to think those objects and the whole external world but shared experience without an external cause. Chapter IV's part is all the pleasanter because Huxley once said that Berkeley's argument was the only thing in metaphysics that had never been and would never be refuted.

Your description of the bookplate is very attractive but I will write to you in a day or two when I can get my wife's ear—she is at present busy with a sick child.

Yours ever

W. B. YEATS

57

Hillcroft, Steep, Petersfield, Hampshire.

[between 5 and 16 January 1926]

My dear Yeats,

Many thanks for your letter. Your deduction from Russell's argument is I think obviously mistaken. The argument is concluded in regard to dreams and hallucinations first on page 172:—

'Error can only arise when we regard the immediate object,

i.e. the sense-datum, as the mark of some physical object': then on pages 193 and 194.

Your friend's action was exactly parallel to Othello's. She acted as though the stone were there, as he acted as though his wife loved Cassio. Their acting thus in no way proves that the stone was there or that Desdemona loved anyone but Othello.

The audience see Othello act as if his wife loved Cassio, just as you saw your friend act as though she lifted a stone. But you did not see the stone and they do not see Desdemona show an adulterous affection for Cassio. No doubt if things which are before the mind were really in the mind, as Berkeley thought, the stone would have the same right to exist in your friend's mind as whatever she was then standing on, but that is the position which you admit that Russell refutes.

An 'illusion' differs from a perception in being entirely private, not shared with others and contradicted by their perceptions. In this it is exactly like a mistake, only it is a mistake of the senses not of the mind. Their mechanism is out of order as, in a mistake, the mind's is.

See also page 70 in Chapter 4. 'We can never truly judge that something exists with which we are not acquainted,' which he [Russell] says is palpably false; it also is false to suppose that anything with which we are acquainted as your friend was acquainted with the missal is known to exist; we must know first whether our acquaintance with it is only acquaintance with the thought of it that has been able to cheat our senses. For to think otherwise would be to confuse, as Russell says, the thing apprehended with the act of apprehension, page 65. Both are distinct and therefore either may exist without the other, as the act of apprehension existed for your friend without the missal. That act induced her to believe the missal actually in her hands when it was not there.

Huxley was an amateur in philosophy like you and me, and made mistakes quite as easily as we do. And philosophers themselves make mistakes, though not quite so easily; they need more apparatus to befool them. Russell had not your view before his mind; he was expounding to an average mind that has neither desire nor inclination to find that what it would call an hallucination might be as real as what it calls real. If he had had your point of view in mind I think he could have turned his argument against it as effectively as against common sense or against Berkeley.

Hoping that you are well and the child quite recovered, and all prospering around you,

Yours ever

T. STURGE MOORE

58*

82 Merrion Square S. Dublin.

16 January [*1926*]

My dear Sturge Moore,

My wife likes your suggested design for Anne's bookplate greatly so go ahead with it.

John Ruskin, while talking with Frank Harris, ran suddenly to the other end of the room, picked up, or seemed to pick up, some object which he threw out of the window. He then explained that it was a tempting demon in the form of a cat. Now if the house cat had come in both cats would have looked alike to Ruskin. (I know this for I once saw a phantom picture and a real picture side by side.) Neither your brother nor Russell gives any criterion by which Ruskin could have told one cat from the other. No doubt if pressed they would have said that if Ruskin's cat was real Harris would have seen it. But that argument amounts to nothing. Dr. Smyllie, a well-known Dublin doctor, made his class see the Indian rope trick by hypnotic suggestion a few years ago. All saw it: whether the suggestion was mental merely or visual makes no difference. Perhaps Russell would say 'a real object' persists, a phantom does not. Shelley pointed out once that the same dream recurs again and again. It is because of these arguments that Eddington, who is a greater

63

mathematician than Russell, and, I think, a sounder philosopher, said lately that all we have a right to say of the external world is that it is a 'shared experience.'

No, on further consideration I feel certain that I shall never be able to write my essay on 'The real existence of Gorgons and Chimæras dire,' and dedicate it to your brother and Russell. I return to Calderón—not only things but 'dreams themselves are a dream.'

Yours sincerely

W. B. YEATS

Things are more or less 'real' according to the extent to which they are capable of being shared with others or ourselves at a different date, but there is no hard and fast line. I think if you enquire you will find that neither your brother nor Russell have in this matter convinced philosophers—at least I was told so at Oxford with some emphasis. So don't let either keep you from reading Gentile, who says 'The external world is so improbable that we go about touching it with our hands to convince ourselves that it exists.'

There is no relation between Ruskin's cat and Desdemona's guilt. Ruskin's cat is a 'sense-datum'—it has weight, colour, shape—whereas D's guilt is false reasoning.

59*

Hillcroft, Steep, Petersfield, Hampshire.

[*after 16 January 1926*]

My dear Yeats,

I will put the bookplate under weigh as soon as I can get clear of my book and have it always in mind. Many thanks.

You don't seem to follow or answer Russell's argument; only to re-state your case. Do you deny that there are such things as hallucinations? Do you think that there are black snakes wriggling on the counterpane of a man who has D.T.? If so, we are only quarrelling about a fact, or a word. If you suppose there is a separate reality for each one of us that is not what we usually mean by reality it is putting a new meaning to the word. Perhaps nothing is real, and we and our experience may be 'such stuff as dreams are made of!' [*sic*]. But we call things real as a matter of fact because of those properties in which they differ from dreams. Everybody supposes that an hallucination in the form of a cat looks to the hallucinated person exactly like a cat. As his experience is entirely private nobody can say anything certain about it except himself. But it belongs to a class of things which experience has come to regard as delusions, like the rope trick. Do you deny that our senses can be deranged and make mistakes, just as our reasoning faculty may, as in Othello's case, make a mistake? If you bang your head against a door you see stars that are not there but swim around you as though they were. The blow has deranged your sense of sight, just as a disease may, or a hypnotic trance, or even a conviction may.

When private experience differs radically from common experience there are differing degrees of probability as to which is wrong. Nobody supposes there is a hard and fast line here, only we all suppose that some private experiences have a very poor chance. And I think Ruskin's cat is one that has a vanishing chance, just as Einstein's special law which contradicts our expectations seems to have a growing chance of superseding the traditional account of experience, but this is because it has been proved in certain instances to tally with carefully controlled observations better than the received account.

If such experiences as Ruskin's cat should ever be found to tally with exact observation they would come out of the class of hallucinations and be ranked as real exterior events. I myself believe that some spirit phenomena will certainly come to be viewed as real as a result of further investigation, but I think that will still leave a large class of hallucinations.

Truth is opposed to error. Nobody supposes that there is no

error at all in the views of up-to-date science; indeed Russell says we now perceive that there is more room for it than used to be supposed, but compared with common-sense views on certain points we suppose that the admixture of error has been very greatly reduced, just as we suppose common sense to make fewer errors than quite private convictions on other points.

Yours ever

T. S. MOORE

60

82 Merrion Square S. Dublin.

26 January [*1926*]

Dear Sturge Moore,

Damn Russell—he is as fine a mathematician as you like, but when he philosophises a politician walking on his hands. I have been amusing myself by drawing conclusions from your brother's argument. Your brother is not a politician but a philosopher. Berkeley and practically all philosophers since have contended that 'sensations' are a part of the human mind and that 'we know nothing but spirits and their relations.' Your brother and his school contend that 'sensations' are 'behind,' not in, the mind.[1] They, like Berkeley, are concerned with *immediate* knowledge: what you write about hallucinations has nothing to do with it. I, so far as I can at the moment see, do not accept your brother's argument—what immediate knowledge have we of that 'behind'? —but it interests me.

Now Ruskin's cat and the house cat are both sensations (or your brother would say each is a 'sense-datum') and therefore both are 'behind' the mind. I do not think your brother would refuse to admit this. I know that his school meets the Berkeleian argument that all things get their form and colour from the

[1] Professor Moore says 'what we actually contended was not this, but that they were "before" the mind, not in it. Yeats has simply made nonsense by substituting "behind" for "before".'

nature of our senses and are therefore only 'appearances' by saying that if a hot object on touching the body produces a cold sensation that cold sensation is 'objective' and that if two people see the same object but differently coloured both colours are 'objective,' from which it obviously follows that Ruskin's cat is 'objective' and from which a whole lot follows which is not scientific materialism but which may, for all that, put so great a part of what the 'realist' considers human thought—vivid imagination of all sorts—outside the mind that it turns that mind, or seems to me to do so at the moment, into the quicksilver at the back of a mirror.

Why should nature create that useless quicksilver? My own belief is that we know nothing but 'spirits and their relations,' but if I could escape from the useless quicksilver [I] would see nothing I care for involved if I had to consider the stream of images ('sense-data,' Ruskin's cat and the house cat), which since Berkeley have seemed a part of the mind, as separate from it.

As to the empiric argument, the 'reality' of Ruskin's cat grows with the number who hear it mew, according to the idealist position, yet reality may be what Napoleon said of history 'a lie that we have agreed on.'

Yours ever

W. B. YEATS

61*

82 Merrion Square S. Dublin.

5 February [1926]

Dear Sturge Moore,

The Times Literary Supplement this week (page 27 column 2) divides possible beliefs about the nature of the external world as follows:—

(1) Everything we perceive 'including so-called illusions, exists in the external world.' (Ruskin's cat and the house cat are real.)

(2) Nothing can exist that is not in the mind as 'an element of experience.' (Neither Ruskin's cat nor the house cat is real.)

(3) There is a physical world which is independent of our minds—'real'—but we can only know it through 'representations' that are part of our mind and quite unlike it.

Russell's point of view is apparently a mixture of (1) and (3) for he holds that 'sense-data' and physical objects are both real but tries to avoid claiming that there are two objectives by saying that 'sense-data' are neither in the mind nor not in the mind. His theory seems to me confused and based on an assumption that he does not prove.

(1) always fascinated me for I learnt it from a Brahman when I was eighteen, and believed it till Blake drove it out of my head. It is early Buddhism and results in the belief, still living in India, that all is a stream which flows on out of human control, one action or thought leading to another, that we ourselves are nothing but a mirror and that deliverance consists in turning the mirror away so that it reflects nothing; the stream will go on but we not know.

(2) This is Zen Buddhism. Shēn-hsiu said (see Waley's *Introduction to the Study of Chinese Painting*, page 221) 'Scrub your mirror lest dust dim it'—I shorten the sentence—but Hui-nēng replied 'Seeing that nothing exists how can the dust dim it?'. Zen art was the result of a contemplation that saw all becoming through rhythm a single act of the mind.

Russell and his school cannot escape from the belief that each man is a sealed bottle. Every man who has studied psychical science by watching his own life knows that we share emotion, thought and image. 'Thought transference' implies a spatial theory of the mind and is a wrong phrase. It is theoretically possible that some vision, like that of the rope trick I described, might expand until it enclosed the whole human race and lasted many years or for ever. At what point, according to Russell's doctrine, does it first coincide with a 'physical object'? Certainly [when?] it has become the world.

(1), (2) and (3) all seem to be tenable: not Russell's compromise. I have come to reject (1) because of my conviction that we can influence events. (3) has to meet all the arguments that have been pressed by idealists and realists alike against a 'physical substratum.' (1) [*sic*: (2)?] This seems to me the simplest and to liberate us from all manner of abstractions and create at once a joyous artistic life.

However when one admits, if one does, that mind which creates all is limited from the start by certain possibilities, one admits Platonic ideas, and so a pre-natal division of the 'unconscious' into two forms of mind. This is a Vedantic thought. However I try always to keep my philosophy within such classifications of thought as will keep it to such experience as seems a natural life. I prefer to include in my definition of water a little duckweed or a few fish. I have never met that poor naked creature H_2O.

I don't want to waste your time and mine by a metaphysical argument but I came to think my letters over-petulant—Russell puts me into a state of incoherence—and that I owed you an explanation.

Yours ever

W. B. YEATS

62

82 Merrion Square S. Dublin.

15 February [1926]

My dear Moore,

The experiments made by J. Ochorowicz in photographing images of the mind were made with the medium Stanislava Tomaczyk (now Mrs. Everard Feilding) at Warsaw and are well known. The other person whose photographs of thought I spoke of was Commandant Darget, who is spoken of with respect by Richet. Richet himself speaks of the impossibility of drawing any distinct line between objective and subjective images. Among Darget's photographs I remember one very distinct and unmistakable of somebody's thought of a walking stick. I met him in Paris before the war but do not know where his results are to be found.

There are not many actual photographs, though quite enough to establish the point for any student who can weigh the value of the testimony, but there is great evidence of other kinds. The distinction between objective and subjective images is to any student of this subject obsolete.

Yours ever

W. B. YEATS

63*

The Shiffolds, Holmbury St. Mary, Dorking.

[after 15 February 1926]

My dear Yeats,

When your first letter reached me I was working at high pressure finishing my book and so could not reply.

You seem to me to have gone back to your original position which you had admitted untenable.

Of the three tenable positions of The Times Literary Supplement reviewer, I suppose my brother believes himself to have smashed both one and two. Three is what he holds to be true. But of course it is necessary to know what one means by it. No appearance can of course be the truth about any object in the senses of being identical with that object or commensurate with that object, but all appearances are true to the object in the sense of being appearances of it, not of something else.

Now you say there may be no object but only the appearance, like an image in a looking-glass. First it would not be like the image in the looking-glass unless there was an object, as we observe both the object and its reflection in the looking-glass. When we remember or imagine the looking-glass simile is no longer applicable. In memory the exposed photographic plate is developed and the image re-appears. In imagination the sensitive photographic plate is no longer a just image, and what actually happens in the brain and how consciousness is connected with the nervous stimulus is entirely unknown. We can neither conceive of nor imagine the truth about it. We can only confess ignorance.

The relation between consciousness and experience cannot be analysed or even conceived in any way. We suppose that the nerves somehow translate or change the commotion caused in them by sensuous stimulants like light or density or sound or smell or flavour into conscious perceptions but where or how this takes place nobody knows.

If you put conceptions like mind or spirit or personality behind awareness of self there is no reason for refusing to put conceptions like matter or space or a space-time continuum behind the appearances of which consciousness is aware. All we immediately experience is the awareness. We are aware of present things and of remembered things which we conclude were present to us before but which are no longer so present, but only a more or less faulty or inadequate reproduction of the effect of their presence is what we are now aware of. We are aware of imagined things sometimes so vividly that we forget they are not really present, as when in thinking of a person we surprise ourselves by suddenly beginning to speak to them as though they were present.

We can form no kind of adequate idea of what takes place. We have present mere experience in which we distinguish three classes, things we term present, things we term remembered, and things we term imagined. We believe they differ from one another above all in actuality. Those we think of as present seem wholly actual, the others have less actuality, diminishing down to none at all. What actuality is we do not know, except that it describes the difference between present objects and memories and imaginations and hallucinations; these last three have little or no actuality.

Now, is there something behind experience? You say 'spirits'; I say I do not know, only the meaning of experience includes 'of'—experience *of something*. What we mean by truth is experience of reality. You say reality is spirits. Why? You have no reason. I say reality is the unknown quality that completes experience which without it can only be partially true but which has many degrees of partial truth, distinguishing Ruskin's cat from the house cat quite clearly as things which no normal experience could confuse. We have no reason that I know of to suppose that the reality behind consciousness is of a different nature to the reality behind appearances; we only know that neither seems the whole truth about itself, but our ignorance does not at all invalidate all those degrees of self-consistency of which we are aware in appearances as well as in consciousness and which we hold must be a part of their reality though not the whole of it. What the other part is of course we cannot form a guess about, at least no reasonable guess, but appearances are almost universally held to belong to a reality vaster in extent and in duration and foreign in nature to the reality behind consciousness. But to what extent vaster and to what degree or in what way foreign we can form no reasonable guess. But there is no more reason to suppose mind real than to suppose matter real; they are on a par.

There, I hope you will see that there is another possibility between materialism and idealism which seems to me at least saner and less presumptuous than either.

Yours ever

T. S. MOORE

64

82 Merrion Square S. Dublin.

17 February [*1926*]

Dear Sturge Moore,

Here is another problem. Richet gives a number of cases of what he calls 'Bilocation.' I have several times come upon such cases. My wife has seen me sitting in my study working when I was in reality—so far as I knew—walking in the street a mile off.

This case seems to me exactly analogous with the 'double vision' studied by your brother. To what image did the 'objective reality' correspond? Is it behind one image and not the other? (Your brother rejects this in the case of double vision.) Is it, let us say, where the thought is? In some cases it has been proved that the thought was where the 'phantasmal' image was. Is it behind both images? Is this 'possibility of sensation,' or whatever it is, spatial? And so on.

If you say the fact that we think of one image as 'phantasmal' decides the matter, we are in great perplexity to decide what we mean by 'phantasmal.' Certainly the 'phantasmal' image is the more isolated, just as 'Ruskin's cat' is isolated—it does not seem to have kittens—but is one bead by itself less real than a bead upon a string?

Yours ever

W. B. YEATS

65*

Friday, 19 February 1926

Dear Yeats,

Most thoughts do not affect photographic plates. If some do, why? All material objects can be photographed. This difference must be explained in order to do away with the difference between subjective and objective. I admit that there are some well-testified occurrences which seem inexplicable; nobody supposes that science is adequate to the universe. But you want to thrust on us an explanation which cannot be proved correct, and would make our problems far more difficult than even they are. You cannot tell us how thought affects the photographic plate? You cannot analyse the occurrence or relate it to others. Science does analyse events and inter-relate them not perfectly or sufficiently but considerably. Why do some thoughts fail to photograph themselves on sensitive plates? That some do cannot prove that this is part of the nature of thought. There may be a common-sense explanation which has not yet been discovered because the cases when thoughts have been so photographed are not sufficiently under control to allow of sequent experiments.

I have not yet read my brother's *Defence of Common Sense* and I cannot decipher all the sentences in your last three letters, and am going to Scotland to lecture for a fortnight on Wednesday, so cannot spare the time just now to look up Richet etc. Besides I am willing to accept evidence about inexplicable phenomena. That is not where the difficulty lies, I think. A question is only philosophical as long as it cannot be sufficiently clearly stated to become scientific. If it were proved that the objective view hitherto held by science was untenable the alternative would not be 'idealism,' I conceive, but merely a larger admission of ignorance. 'Idealism' has to explain away science. Why should experience correspond to the laws of perspective if the distance between me and the house over there is not objective? That distance causes the sense-data of that house to look so small that I can cover it with my thumb nail. If I walk along the road they become such a vast aggregate that I can go inside and walk about in it. I can watch a man who is six feet high walk along the road till he becomes a midget's size and goes into the house. I can watch him return and ask him if he diminished in size with the sense-data I received from him, and I believe him when he says he is certain he did not, as I myself have been there and back and remained the same sense-data the whole time.

If the common-sense view were disproved it must be in some way such as Einstein disproves Newton, leaving Newton true as far as controlled observations had approved him, only contradicting speculative deductions from there.

With regard to idealism: have the words 'thought' and 'mind' meanings apart from a supposed relation to a three-dimensional universe? These words differentiate certain experiences from others: if both are *thought* how is this observed difference to be accounted for? If reality is merely in the mind, how differentiate what according to the common-sense view is in the mind from those things that on the same view are in space?

Science and common sense are founded on observation of these differences. If there is no such difference how explain their practical efficacy? As Russell says, we now know that we know so little about reality that it seems marvellous that so small an amount of knowledge should have given us such very considerable power over events and sense-data. If, as I think, the meaning of the words 'thought' and 'mind' merely describes these relations to an objective universe, if there is no such universe they have no meaning. We absolutely ignore[1] the nature of the connection between *mind and thought* and the *cause of sense-data*. There must be some connection. When it is discovered we shall be able to advance in these enquiries; until then we have to content ourselves with making the statement of our ignorance more and more precise till it finally becomes knowledge.

Imagination so vivid as to produce sense-data equal to those received from objects is an inconceivable thing that occurs according to common sense. Common sense prefers to class 'Ruskin's cat' with imaginations rather than to suppose it a hiatus in the chain of controlled observations. It is not a mere question between a bead loose and one on a string. The string is a perfect necklace of beads. And the loose bead is not certainly a bead; it may be an imagination of one, and we know that there are a great many imaginary beads and have been very careful not to thread any into our necklace which now consists only of beads that have been proved to be different from imaginations in that they can be passed from hand to hand and counted on behaving always in the same way. Whereas imaginations let you down somewhere or other if you play freely with them and try to count on their behaviour.

Whatever may be the actual nature of reality, we have most

---

[1] i.e. we are ignorant of, 'ignore' being used in the French or the archaic sense.

cogent reasons for supposing that it does correspond with exact science as far as exact science goes. What happens to it before and after we do not know, but we have been to and fro that observed distance so often that we shall not believe now that there is no difference between it and an imagination which only rivals the vividness of reality occasionally or on a single occasion.

Does 'idealism' mean anything? is the question to which no affirmative answer has been given that has not been countered by those who answer it in the negative. To suppose that it means anything is therefore a highly speculative position, as all controlled observation is against that view. Things have been observed, and well attested, that have not yet been controlled. To the experience of them apparently as real as any other no counterproof[1] from the known conditions for their occurrence is yet to hand. But there is no reason to suppose that that counterproof when discovered will not consist with all the knowledge hitherto furnished with counterproofs which we call science.

That is, as clearly as I can put it, the case against 'idealism' but there is nothing to prevent the values usually confused with the idealist view according with the common-sense view far better than with any so-called spiritual view. I believe these spiritual values do accord with common sense.

Yours ever

T. S. MOORE

66*

82 Merrion Square S. Dublin.

[*between 19 February and 11 March 1926*]

Dear Moore,

We have got too far into detail: to answer you I would have to write a book. However, I will make a few suggestions.

---

[1] Professor Moore points out that his brother habitually used 'counterproof' in the exact opposite of its sense, i.e. to mean 'confirmation' instead of 'refutation.'

(1) The photographing of images of the mind and the rarity of the event do not give me great difficulty, but then I am not a realist.

(2) When I described an extension of your brother's problem of the double visual images to cases where the two images are many miles, perhaps the width of the world, apart, I forgot to say that in one well-attested case the more 'phantasmal' image was photographed. Again, not being a realist I am not upset by the fact.

(3) I now suggest to you another problem. There are many well-attested cases of prevision. Just as the double images seem to imply a spaceless reality, these seem to imply a reality which is timeless, a transcendental ego. Again, not being a realist these rare cases give me little trouble.

You speak of the difficulties which you feel in reconciling perspective with any system which sees reality as being and the world as thought created. You will find perspective fully discussed in Berkeley's *New Theory of Vision* and elsewhere, and that one of his principal arguments for immaterialism is founded upon it. It is a very abstract and technical argument.

You have listened too much to B. Russell in his electioneering moods—the Plain Man has nothing to do with the matter. The Plain Man, even when magnified into a man of science, would be very little content with your brother's last conception of reality as a bundle of 'possibilities of sensation' (possibilities are immaterial, by the bye, till they are transformed into something else). To your brother and B. Russell all the sense-data—the only thing the Plain Man cares for—are mainly created by the mind. That is to say the world in which the possibilities become real— the only reality—does not exist until it has been thought.

You say 'Idealism has to explain away science.' But that has nothing to do with the matter. (We are not compelled to write in the younger liberal reviews.) Read Eddington's essay on *Science, Religion and Reality*. He shows exactly why the discoveries of science can never affect the problem of reality.

By the bye, the conundrum which I have put to you in vain in these letters was I find familiar to Professor James. An essay on 'realism' in *The Encyclopaedia of Religion and Ethics* said that he contended that 'there is no specific character of mental things, the difference between mental and physical being one of context and arrangement.' He was familiar with the evidence of psychical research which neither B. Russell nor your brother has, I think, studied.

Yours ever

W. B. YEATS

Remember that the bug, the bear, the beetle and the bat are great electioneers.

67

Hillcroft, Steep, Petersfield, Hampshire.

[*before 11 March 1926*]

My dear Yeats,
    You do not answer my arguments and I do not answer yours, partly because they are so difficult to read. I never said anything about the plain man but to start from him as the normal majority; he has made language, and thought for him is, in contra-distinction to objective reality, an interpretation of it or an imagination based on it in some unknown way. Thought means *this*; then if you give it a new meaning by saying that everything is thought you want new terms for the two controlled observations which were distinguished in language as thought and objective reality: but by using thought to cover both you only fog the mind.
    Berkeley had resort to God to explain objective reality; God went on thinking and so his thoughts remained just as the objective reality does; in fact there was only a verbal difference between the two. It matters little whether I call a tree a tree or God's thought of a tree if both have exactly the same properties.

The only objection to doing the latter is that it is less simple and less concise.

The word 'sense-datum' implies something received and something given: sense is the medium of communication or conveyance. This is implied in the common-sense view—reality gives and I receive through my senses. Reality is presupposed just as I am; neither can exist without the other for me, though I have cogent reasons to think that reality has existed before me, and will or may exist after.

This I take it is my brother's position.

I have read Eddington's essay and greatly admired it. It entirely accords with the common-sense view that science is a description of those properties of reality which can be abstracted, but the remainder, which Eddington sums up under the head Actuality, remains intractable to scientific method and contains most of the values of experience. In his last sentences he wavers, I think unnecessarily, by quoting St. John because he has no time to discuss in what sense he is using the word 'made' or in what sense the 'word' could be in the beginning. Words arrived, according to science, at rather a late period in our world. And we have no right to use this word 'word' in an entirely new and unrelated sense without the very strictest definition of that new meaning.

Silverdale
11 March 1926

When in Cambridge a week ago I asked my brother about the 'double image' spoken of in his recent essay. He said he had no such phenomenon as you speak of in mind but merely the ordinary result of fatigue or drink that makes you see things doubled. He also said I was right about Berkeley's view being only verbally different from the common-sense scientific view, because God's thoughts for him exactly correspond to what is called external or objective reality.

He also agreed that your view needs to define the difference

79

between Ruskin's cat that only seemed real to one mind and things that constantly seem real to all normal folk. There is a difference, therefore they cannot be said to be the same. And you must find a definition that, unlike Berkeley's, is not merely verbally different from the view that calls one subjective and the other objective.

Gordon Bottomley, in whose house we are now staying, asks to be very kindly remembered to you.

Yours ever

T. S. MOORE

68

82 Merrion Square S. Dublin.

12 March [*1926*]

My dear Sturge Moore,

I am greatly interested to find you have talked these things over with your brother whose work, the little of it I know, has been of great value to me. I agree with what he says about the later Berkeley, who was a Platonist. My Berkeley is the Berkeley of the *Commonplace Book*, and it is this Berkeley who has influenced the Italians. The essential sentence is of course 'things only exist in being perceived,' and I can only call that perception God's when I add Blake's 'God only acts or is in existing beings or men.' However I don't want to labour this, which is quite an old point.

All my letters to you have been the result of my conviction that psychical research has undermined every current statement of the realist position which goes beyond the last three pages of your brother's essay in *Contemporary British Philosophy*.

It seems to me entirely arbitrary on your brother's [part]—of course I query if he did make this distinction—to distinguish between the neighbouring double images caused by drunkenness and the double images which have some unknown cause and are separated perhaps by many miles, especially as both images can, as I believe, affect the photographic plate.

Again, if I understand you rightly, he thinks 'real objects' are 'constantly' visible, while Ruskin's cat is only visible to one. This is exactly what my psychic experience denies. A dream—Ruskin's cat—is frequently collective and has affected the photographic plate; and, upon the other hand, there is the form of 'hallucination' which causes the temporary disappearance (they may even cease to affect the photographic plate, if one well-attested case can be relied on) of real objects—the house cat.

The present realist argument breaks down because we have no longer the right to say that there is any image of the mind peculiar to one person: something of it is peculiar, as something of the images we call physical is peculiar, and that is all we can say. It becomes necessary to consider that all minds may make under certain circumstances a single mind. I am convinced that the diary of any psychic investigator is sufficient answer to any such philosophy as that in *Problems of Philosophy*. I think your brother to be consistent must not only consider double images separated in space but double images separated in time (prevision). His 'permanent possibilities' remain, but how define their 'permanence,' and are they independent of the perceiving mind in the light of these new facts? Of course he may not believe that these are facts at all.

Yours ever

W. B. YEATS

69*

82 Merrion Square S. Dublin.

14 March [*1926*]

My dear Moore,

Your brother's latest thought is in *A Defence of Common Sense* (*Contemporary British Philosophy*, second series). He argues that we can be certain of nothing but the presence before the mind of 'sense-data.' He examines an example of sense-data—a case of double vision—and argues that we cannot know what the 'sense-data' represent but shows that he prefers Mill's theory that 'material things' are 'permanent possibilities of sensation.' He thinks 'it just possible' that this is the true explanation but goes no further.

'Permanent possibilities' in this case can only be the mathematic possibilities discussed by Eddington. These are as near infinite as anything we can imagine. In that case, is there any limit to possible dimensions, for instance? But in any case what decides that this or that possibility is to become actual? Surely the human mind. The choice between almost infinite possibilities is surely almost infinite creations. In so far therefore as Time and Space are deduced from our sense-data we are the creators of Time and Space.

When I wrote my first letter I did not know how slight was my quarrel with your brother. My acceptance of his *Refutation of Idealism* (the title is merely politics, for he explains in the essay itself that he does not claim to have refuted idealism) was an ironical acceptance, and meant to get you to admit my real point. 'Ruskin's cat' is a sense-datum—we are aware of it as of say the colour blue—and if it is a sense-datum so are other images in the mind, say dream-images. I wanted to remind you that 'Ruskin's cat,' granted certain extrinsic conditions, could be photographed. D'Ochorowicz photographed an image in the mind of his medium and the arm of a form created by suggestion. I have seen also such photographs taken by another investigator. Ruskin's cat could have been seen and heard by others, granted certain conditions. I have again and again tested the visibility and audibility of mind-created forms.

I want to widen the issue so that instead of sense-data in the narrow sense of the words we have to deal with the whole of that which the mind knows. If we accept the belief that the cause or underlying reality of all is 'permanent possibility' (why does your brother, who is generally so sceptical, call these possibilities 'material' instead of using some non-committal word?) we have still almost infinite intellectual, emotional and bodily creations. If however your brother's scepticism gets the upper hand with him and others then we have almost infinite creations out of an unknown something and we are almost back at Berkeley, for Berkeley is probably the next step.

Personally I believe there is a Matrix but that Matrix seems to me living and active, not a mere logical possibility. But that is a long story. It is a blow against my blow.

I have been unjust to Bertrand Russell: his politics infuriated me. I could not read philosophy till my big book was written. Those who gave me material forbid me to do so; they feared, I think, that if I did do so I would split up experience till it ceased to exist. When it was written (though the proofs had yet to come) I started to read. I read for months every day Plato and Plotinus. Then I started on Berkeley and Croce and Gentile. You introduced me to your brother's work and to Russell, and I found Eddington and one or two others for myself. I am still however anything but at my ease in recent philosophy. I find your brother extraordinarily obscure.

There has been a horrible row at the Abbey. Republicans tried to rush the stage on Thursday, and on Saturday morning sent armed men to kidnap our chief actor. Luckily he was not at home. All yesterday we kept the players in the theatre under police protection. The cause of the row is a play of Casey's against war and civil war for which every seat has been full—a great play, like a Russian novel.

Yours ever

W. B. YEATS

I have now dealt with your main points though not all. Your assumption that 'Ruskin's cat' unlike the 'house cat' is an image without an object is quite impossible.

70

Hillcroft, Steep, Petersfield, Hampshire.

21 March 1926

My dear Yeats,

My brother did not deny your facts; he only said that he had not referred to them in his essay. Any application of his argument to them is therefore yours not his. He did not know your evidence. And I think such evidence would need in his view a very perfect counterproof before it could be argued from to support a philosophical concept.

The sentence you quote from Berkeley's *Commonplace Book* would seem to reflect a view held I believe by Leibnitz which supposes that there is nothing but experience, mere experience, no person and no external reality. You yourself only exist while you perceive that you perceive. This amounts to saying that neither matter nor spirit possesses unknown qualities, for which presumption there seems to be no reason save that it saves us from making suppositions about things we do not know, which is even probably a rash use of thought, but observe it is itself such a supposition, and a negative one. But on this view thoughts we have not thought will not exist till we think them. Therefore there is no unknown truth. I think this view is also open to the objection that it empties language of meanings without which we never do think.

By a counterproof I mean that a phenomenon is never scientifically described until the conditions are known in which it will certainly recur. Evidence that it has occurred, however good, is not sufficient to enable science to describe it fully; when it can be reproduced or predicted then it becomes part of the body of scientific knowledge.

The difficulty about your double images would seem to be that they cannot be examined; we have to accept the report of somebody though that report cannot be verified. Even if they have been photographed this is still the case, as some one must tell us this is the photograph of a mental image. We ourselves cannot compare it to the mental image it is a photograph of. So when a lot of people see the same thing all we know is that they say they see the same thing, and we know how easily people can use the same words to describe quite different experiences.

To found a philosophical theory on such grounds is the wildest speculation. Einstein's mathematical calculations were only accepted when definite predictions made on the strength of them were borne out by astronomical observations. Before that happened his calculations only furnished an hypothesis; and, as far as I know, psychical research can only furnish evidence of occurrences and hypotheses which contradict or conflict with others that have and can furnish the counterproof which psychical research can as yet, in very few cases, even pretend to furnish. Everybody admits that there are unexplained phenomena of which the concomitants are almost totally unknown, but to build a theory on such ground or to suppose that phenomena of which the concomitants are known and can be counterproved are nullified by such evidence is wild speculation and carries no weight. My brother need not either accept or reject your facts, he may suspend judgement pending the production of their counterproofs.

Yours ever

T. S. MOORE

71*

82 Merrion Square S. Dublin.

[*before 29 March 1926*]

Dear Sturge Moore,

Forty years ago the Society for Psychical Research succeeded in transferring mental images (numbers, geometrical forms, simple drawings) between two people (1) in the same room, (2) in different rooms, (3) in different towns. From that moment all philosophy based upon the isolation of the individual mind became obsolete.

The ecclesiastics of the mechanical philosophy met this and all evidence of psychical research by the demand that no fact of this kind could be accepted until, as you put it, 'the conditions are known in which it will certainly recur.' This was an evasion, for psychical facts belong to mind which never does the same thing in exactly the same way twice because all moments of being are unique. They in fact demanded that mind should become mechanism before they would consider its action.

No two people see exactly the same world of sense-data ever, whether these sense-data are mental or physical images; nor does one person see the same world twice. The material may be the same but the pattern is different.

I read a book of Catholic apologetics a few years ago which contended with much proof that the Church had not condemned Galileo's doctrine but merely Galileo for teaching it before he could fully prove it. It is a subconscious trick which must tempt every creed which is incompatible with some fact to perpetually demand to have that fact proved over and over again. There need be no end to this process, especially if the ecclesiastics, scientific or theological, do not look at the proofs.

The belief that all is experience does not mean that there is no truth unknown to us for there are unknown minds, but it does mean that there is no truth where there is no mind to know it.

I have just got Whitehead's *Science and the Modern World*. He collaborated with B. Russell in books of mathematical philosophy. I think I shall find myself in fair agreement with him. He asks what 'reality' is to be assigned to 'nature,' and adds that Berkeley 'states it to be the reality of ideas in the mind,' and then says 'a complete metaphysic which has attained to some notion of mind and to some notion of ideas may perhaps adopt this view' but does not wish for the moment 'to ask so fundamental a question.' For the moment he advocates 'objectivism,' that is to say substantially what I described to you as the philosophy of early

Buddhism, as distinguished from that of Zen (which is, I think, Berkeleian). Do not therefore look on the matter as a closed issue.

Yours ever

W. B. YEATS

Whitehead describes the mechanical theory thus:—'The sense-data or sensations are projected by the mind so as to clothe appropriate bodies in external nature. . . . The poets are entirely mistaken. . . . Nature is a dull affair, soundless, scentless, colourless; merely the hurrying of material, endlessly, meaninglessly.' (*Science and the Modern World*, page 77.)

72

Hillcroft, Steep, Petersfield, Hampshire.

29 March 1926

My dear Yeats,

I have again been away from home or would have replied to yours earlier. You cannot have it both ways; if everything is mind or thought, the recurrences observed by science and on which it is founded characterise thought and mind which must have at least so much regularity as these employ. So your distinction between psychical and physical facts has no ground. Mind must include all the mechanism observed or conceived. As to whether the same person sees the same world twice, science does not suppose that a person ever sees exactly the same world twice, and the very high degree of similarity which exists between one moment of thought and another must be a character of thought if it is not a character of the object thought about. For science the facts are proved when they are seen as parts of a sequence and exist whenever and wherever that sequence exists. No fact is yet seen as a part of a complete sequence including all others, so that no fact is fully proved for science.

I am afraid you are wrong, and the view that there is no truth is and has been held and obtains a fresh vigour from the quantum theory.

I have the greatest respect for Whitehead, whose mind is more philosophical and less polemical than B. Russell's and whose character seems to be more benignant.

It is admitted by my brother and all that school that the common-sense view they prefer is not finally proved; they only deny that idealism can be proved and assert that the balance of probability is against it. No answer has been found to the most fundamental questions. No sequence yet observed arranges all the types of fact known.

The passage you quote from Whitehead in your P.S. appears to me misleadingly poetical or rhetorical. Appearances are as real as the object and the object cannot be 'by us' perceived without them. The difference is that whereas appearances are conditioned by our faculties, any disease in which distorts them, the object is not so conditioned and can only be deduced abstractly from them; the object is in this sense unknown, i.e. unperceived. Its presence is only implied in our conception of appearances which cannot be so well explained on any other hypothesis.

The transference of thought may be physical in the cases of telepathy just as it is physical by means of speech, books or letters. There is no reason that I know of for supposing it to be effected without physical mechanism, or for supposing all minds to be part of one mind sometimes conscious of one another, sometimes not. *Mind* implies *consciousness*, therefore when it is unconscious there is no proof of its existence. What is an unconscious living mind? What meaning can be given to the words?

Yours ever

T. S. MOORE

73

82 Merrion Square S. Dublin.

31 March [*1926*]

My dear Moore,

My complaint about the claim to 'control' psychic experiments is that the men who make the claim want the living bird to behave like the wooden bird in a Swiss clock. Of course there are always 'sequences' but those of mind are not those of mechanism.

Read Whitehead's *Science and the Modern World*. I have now read the greater part of it and so far it seems to me my own point of view. He proves, as I think, that the mechanical theory of the world is untrue (though it works, like other untrue things) and substitutes a theory of organism. It is concentrated logic throughout and has the same intensity of thought—which is Beauty—that I find in Gentile. He is of course realist, but the difference between his point of view and that of Gentile does not seem to me of much moment until one gets to ultimates, and one does not do that in this book. Perhaps it is not great even then. It would not arise at all unless Whitehead were to insist that his world of 'eternal' objects, by which he means colours, sounds and so on, could remain were there no 'mind' present, and I judge from the sentence I quoted and from his whole doctrine of organism that he certainly does not mean this as he understands mind. Organism without mind—'choice'—in some sense would be mechanism.

He seems to me among other things to give Ruskin's cat all the consideration it can reasonably expect. To Whitehead, as to Berkeley, there is no 'physical substratum,' no 'permanent possibility of sensation' behind the 'sense-data.' The point at issue, if it is at issue, is the independence of these 'sense-data' from 'mind.' The house cat and Ruskin's eat can lie down together in either case.

Of course there have been claims, which no one who has studied the facts has so far accepted to the best of my belief, to explain 'transference of thought' by the mechanical theory, just as there have been much more successful attempts to explain the double images seen by the drunkard. But, like your brother in the matter of the drunkard's images, I think that cannot affect the question philosophically.

An Irish priest surprised me on Monday night. He said: 'Bertrand Russell is a prig and he is not the big man people think

him, but there is a big man behind him—Moore of Cambridge.
The pity is that Moore's mind is analytical and analytical alone.'

Yours ever

W. B. YEATS

I do not attempt to answer your argument as that would need
a long, detailed exposition. I refer you to Whitehead. There is
no 'object' in the sense in which you use that word—that is
the point.

P.S. Of course there is no 'unconscious living mind,' nor is there
—though much science seems to claim it—a 'thinking un-
consciousness.'

I mis-stated your brother in my last letter but one (through bad
sight probably). He did [not] say 'material' but 'permanent
possibilities of sensation.' When B. Russell names such 'possibilities' (his conception is not very different if I remember
rightly) 'physical objects' he is electioneering.

74

Hillcroft, Steep, Petersfield, Hampshire.

20 May 1926

Dear Yeats,

I enclose a rough first sketch for your daughter Anne's bookplate, so that I need not go further with it if the main idea of it
does not please your wife and self.

It represents a girl, younger or older according to choice,
dancing in a single half-transparent garment in the light of a
more than half moon on a rocky islet in an animated but not
rough sea. The shape of the moon sets the tune for those of the
child's dress, the light on the rocks and for the waves of the sea;
the tower rocks in the same way, [to] keep time with the frame.
The girl is not only dancing but curtseying to the moon. I think
it gives opportunity for very pretty engraving work.

Please return it soon and say whether you wish me to proceed or think out another.

I have now read my brother's essay on his position in *Contemporary British Philosophy*.

I think you did not see that before you could take advantage of his hesitation over the analysis of the relation of sense-data to the object you have first to answer his arguments for thinking that it is true that objects truly exist.

I have not yet got hold of Whitehead's book and hope to some day.

Yours sincerely

T. STURGE MOORE

P.S. I hope the children are both in flourishing health once more.

75

Thoor Ballylee, Gort, Co. Galway.

27 May [*1926*]

My dear Sturge Moore,

Make the dancing girl about eighteen. I want my daughter Anne to think of this bookplate as a 'grown-up' bookplate while she is a child and to continue to use it when she is grown-up. The design will be very fine if you keep it severe like my wife's bookplate, which is magnificent. My wife asks me to say that Anne is going to be tall and slight, which no doubt means that she wants the dancing girl to look as much as possible like that admirable faun or stag springing from the broken tower. I must not confuse your symbolism: that beast is the dæmon, which Anne is not. I thank you for the fine design, which I return under a different cover.

Now your philosophic point. I do not, for the moment at any rate, quarrel with your brother's suggestion that 'sense-data' or sensations have underlying them 'a permanent possibility.' I do not think the word 'permanent' adds anything however. In so far as my chair is permanent it is obvious that there is or was a permanent possibility of that chair. The statement that sensations, or 'sense-data,' have underlying them a 'possibility' is Plotinus. He shows that matter has neither colour, scent, nor magnitude, and finally defines it as the 'indeterminate,' which possesses however the possibility of being shaped. He also defines it as 'the alien,' which is Croce's position—an idealist position as distinct from your brother's realism—for Croce describes matter as created by 'intellect' from the mental images by its imposing upon those images the abstract conception of the external.

My quarrel is not with your brother but with Bert Russell who seems to accept your brother's position and yet describes the 'possibilities' as 'physical objects'—which is nonsense. I call this electioneering because it is an attempt to get the support of 'the physical substratum' people, and he knows quite well that their theory is dead.

In the seventeenth century people said [that] our senses are responsible for colour, scent and sound, and that colour, scent and sound are 'appearances' but that mass and movement really exist. In the eighteenth century one or two men pointed out that mass and movement are just as much 'appearances,' because the invention of our senses, as colour, scent and sound. Then a little later is was discovered that the organs themselves—the organs as observed as objects of science—are part of the 'appearances': we see the eye through the eye. From that moment we were back in ancient philosophy and must deduce all from the premises known to Plato.

The points most of my fantasies and extravagances were meant to suggest are not that your brother's 'possibilities' do not exist— why quarrel with a phantom, as Plotinus calls matter?—but that images of the mind and images of sense must have a common root (your brother's claim that Ruskin alone could see his cat is not founded on fact) and that whatever their cause or substratum that substratum is not fixed at one spot in space. As Whitehead has pressed both points I refer you to him for proof.

Read Whitehead, and from that go to Stephen MacKenna's
Plotinus and to the *Timaeus*. What Whitehead calls 'the three
provincial centuries' are over. Wisdom and Poetry return.

Yours ever

W. B. YEATS

I do not understand your argument that science can solve
problems of philosophy. I do not know any philosophers—unless
mathematicians who mean mathematics when they say science—
who think that science can solve a philosophical problem or
philosophy a scientific one. Science can certainly free philosophers from predilections created by bad science (Ruskin only
could see the cat, etc.) but that is a different matter.

76

Thoor Ballylee, Gort, Co. Galway.

9 June [*1926*]

My dear Sturge Moore,
    The only books in the house are Doughty's *Arabia*, Plotinus
and some bad detective stories and a French play, so I cannot look
up those passages in your brother. I do not think however that
they affect my criticism of his position.
    I see two pictures on the wall; one picture vanishes when I go
nearer. I contend that both or neither are 'sense-data,' both or
neither are related to his external sensations. He makes what I
consider an abstract distinction. He seems to consider that the
picture that does not vanish is the partial manufacture of the
mechanism of the eye and so different from the other. That
position seems to me impossible. The mechanism of the eye is
itself a 'sense-datum' and so in need of explanation and not itself
an explanation.
    Furthermore I object to the term 'sense-datum' which is the
invention of people who saw a casual relation between sense-
mechanism and the images, or sounds etc., and so to confuse the

93

issue was brought into philosophy, which sees no such relation.
The difference between the dream-image (phantom picture) and
the 'sense-image' is an apparent difference of continuity. (The
phantom comes and goes suddenly, may appear to several at
once, but usually is seen by one and not seen by the person next,
and so on.) But no difference of continuity permits one to say
that at a certain point the increase of continuity involves
the presence of something (external stimulus) hitherto not
there.

Your brother sees a difference of kind, not of degree, because
he cannot rid his mind of the now obsolete sense-corked bottle
of personality. The moment one considers all the images, sense-
images, dream-images, mind-images, as forming a single existence
one is forced to concede an equal reality to the conceptual ideas,
'continuity,' 'difference,' 'change,' and so on; and the ancient
pair Intellect and Imagination stand face to face. Your brother's
conviction that 'we know nothing but the sense-data' broadens,
'we know' and 'sense-data' take on meaning, till it becomes
Ancient Philosophy. We have had to add 'value' ('the bad,'
'the good,' of Plotinus) because neither ideas nor images are
equal in importance, and perhaps 'matter,' (the 'indeterminate'
of Plotinus) the opposite of value, and so to create the ancient
quaternary.

Your brother does not systematise because he has got himself
involved in a compromise between 'the objectivist' and the
'idealist' positions, which prevents thought owing to its central
fallacy—the sealed bottle. Your brother's belief that two images
of 'the same object' are equally real refutes the theory of an
object at a fixed point in space (and so every current conception
of matter) even without my psychical evidence. If there is an
external 'substratum' Whitehead suggests that it is for every
'sense-datum' the entire ambient—the 'Heavenly circuit' of
Plotinus. All is in all.

Yours ever

W. B. YEATS

94

77*

82 Merrion Square S. Dublin.

16 June [*1926*]

My dear Sturge Moore,

I am in Dublin for Senate and have spent all the time I could give to those pages 202 to 206 of your brother's. He has less gift of expression than any other able man who ever lived. At first I felt as if I was reading 'And they danced till the gunpowder ran out of their heels.' Then I put it into Ruskin's mouth and I understood it better.

'My cat in a *certain sense* really exists. Yet some philosophers have denied this. I have seen it. I have felt its weight. I think it scratched me. Other people have seen such cats. The housemaid saw, in her own room with the door shut, a black cat very like mine and this vanished too. But then I admit that I do not know what it is to see or to weigh. In a *certain sense* it was nearer than the mantelpiece, but then there might have been two images and both images might have been nearer. However there have been philosophers who denied that it was nearer in a *certain sense*. They were clearly wrong and of course no philosopher has been able to hold such views consistently.'

Yours ever

W. B. YEATS

78*

Hillcroft, Steep, Petersfield, Hampshire.

18 June 1926

My dear Yeats,

You have no inkling of my brother's argument. His first two propositions state that we know that a great many things which are not sense-data exist, and then you say that he thinks 'that we know nothing but sense-data.' It is all moonshine and nonsense. If you want to confute him you must make a proposition that is not self-contradictory which conflicts with his two first propositions. He says you cannot. When you say that seeing two pictures on the wall when only one is there is as good proof of the existence of two pictures as if both were on the wall you contradict yourself, because you admit there is only one on the wall. You make a distinction between what you know to exist and an illusion of sense and deny it at the same time. That is to make two contradictory propositions both of which cannot be true. It is not a question as to what happens to be fashionable among intellectuals, but as to whether there is a case that can be stated without involving a contradiction. Fools follow fashions in thought as in other things and then they think because they are very many they must needs be right as well as strong.

The argument about double images is concerned only with the implications of what we know to be true, their analysis, not with their truth. This analysis is very difficult and has not been satisfactorily made but you cannot start out on it until the phenomena to be analysed are admitted to exist truly. And if you deny their existence (as you do) you make a self-contradictory proposition.

He brings sense-data in only in showing the difficulties of the analysis; they do not affect the propositions that many people and many objects truly exist and have existed. This is what we know; what that knowledge involves and implies is another question, to which my brother believes no certainly true answer has yet been given. He shows then the difficulties in the way of accepting three which he thinks it just barely possible may turn out to be true. But he does not think any one of them has been proved. Speculate as much as you like, turn out as many hypotheses as you can, but don't imagine that because they please you they are therefore true or ascertained; they are in this respect quite baseless.

If you admit that common sense would conclude that there was only one picture on the wall when you saw two you contradict your statement that there was equal evidence for both pictures. Even if you only refer to common sense to scorn, deny and flout it, by referring to it at all you admit that it exists and, therefore, that many other persons and objects exist with certain relations between them and that to talk of them all as 'mind' and 'thought' is to talk nonsense. You may not notice that you have admitted this but if you follow my brother's argument you will realise it. And the same applies to Ruskin's cat.

The review of Whitehead's book in *The New Criterion* makes it quite clear that you must have misunderstood him also, for one of the passages quoted is a brief statement of my brother's argument, and besides Whitehead is said to call himself a 'realist.' You seem to have supposed that it was materialism, which has been dead and buried for thirty years, that you were arguing against. Whitehead's theory seems to be a parallel variant to Russell's mind-plus-matter stuff as a substratum to both mental and material existence. This of course both in Russell and Whitehead is pure speculation, an hypothesis presented not as proved but as suggesting new lines of investigation and harmonising certain observed discrepancies brought forward by relativity and the quantum theory, but [it] would offer no kind of basis to Croce or Bergson or, I suppose, to Gentile whose mistakes are prior to and supposed corrected in the positions of Whitehead, B. Russell and my brother.

Your second letter has just come to hand. It is to be supposed that the truth is difficult to apprehend and expound; those who find it easy probably deceive themselves and those who make it seem easy to others deceive their neighbours. If it were not difficult philosophy would become a science. Science before it became certain and could furnish a counterproof was called philosophy. As soon as the answer to a question is an experiment it ceases to be philosophy and becomes science. But the simplest and most fundamental questions that can be asked can not be answered by experiments; with these philosophers still wrestle with a highly technical apparatus of logic which is in itself difficult to understand. If one does not understand it, it is better to say so rather than to gibe at it.

The dialectics of my brother, like those in some of the dialogues of Plato, seem cumbrous and confusing because he omits no single step as obvious: and obviously he must not do so because he is arguing against those who make the simplest and most fundamental mistakes, and they make them merely because they did not follow all the steps entailed because it seemed fastidious to do so; therefore they jump and come croppers.

It needs a very considerable effort and some familiarity with thinking at so slow a pace before one can can fall into step and appreciate the truth of the minute points made. Literature, especially poetry, works in an opposite way, flies rather than crawls, and so to be good at poetry is itself a handicap in philosophy. Many philosophers and most amateurs are only interested in the imaginative aspects of speculation; the search for truth bores them stiff. They are fertile in hypotheses but build on the sand of many treacherous assumptions. They therefore appeal to fashion not to reason and have their giddy day and then are superseded. But the search for truth goes on bringing more and more of experience within the reach of science. It is like all pioneering a lonely job and makes little show in the world which it nevertheless transforms willy-nilly.

That is I belive the position, but you are I think quite mistaken in thinking that Whitehead takes up a different position to my brother about 'Ruskin's cat' or about 'two pictures seen where only one is.' Whitehead's book seems to be an exposition of the evil practical effects of the materialism which was so fashionable thirty years ago and points out how much more room modern realism leaves for morality and religion. In these deductions my brother would refuse to follow him very far at any rate.

The drawing is advancing and I shall soon send it.

Yours ever

T. S. MOORE

P.S. Did you recognise my authorship of the article on the first page of *The Times Literary Supplement* for June 3rd on *The Essence of Verse*?

79

82 Merrion Square S. Dublin.

23rd June [1926]

My dear Sturge Moore,

To reply to you adequately would take several hours. If I answer your letters I must be content to skim the surface. I did not say one picture existed and the other did not. Both or neither exist: that is my point.

The Realist ('objectivist') thinks both do: the Idealist ('subjectivist') thinks neither does. Whitehead describes himself in effect as, provisionally, for dialectical convenience, a realist, but in one passage suggests that his ultimate position is idealist. I think that my own position is more realist than idealist. I do not however see any final contradiction.

Plotinus saw the creation of ideas as an act that did not take place in time, an act that had no beginning. I certainly have not read your brother carefully. My special experience has shown me that the barrier which he assumes between images of sense and of the mind does not exist. I think therefore that he is not an author who has for me a special value. It is nothing to me that my special experience is not yet shared by the majority of teachers in universities (which is what is meant by 'proved'). What matters to me is that it is my experience. Your brother in that essay

99

seems to give a validity to 'common sense' which it may not deserve, though of course we must discover why 'common sense' thinks these things, and in any case I am convinced that common sense, granted a special experience, puts the two cats, to 'a certain extent' as your brother would say, on an equality. Certainly neither common sense nor any other sense, granted that experience, justifies the belief that one cat and not the other has an external root. Your brother has not given the slightest reason for believing in this root in one case and not the other.

When the housemaid says her prayers after seeing a 'phantom' cat her common sense affirms its real existence just as much as mine, if I had said 'one picture was on the wall,' would have affirmed the real existence of that picture, and neither affirmation may have objective philosophical value.

It may be of great importance to weigh the old conviction of the flatness and stillness of the earth, and Blake thought that still and flat earth true, the other a falsification of reason. Does not your brother contradict common sense, just as the astronomers did, when he suggests that both his 'images' have the like reality, which implies that matter is spatially fixed?

Your argument seems to be that I must not make this point because your brother is not sure of his. He has however made the statement or suggestion and I have the right to show that it is incompatible with what I think his general theory or general suggestion. If I still misunderstand your brother's first two propositions I wish you would put them plainly for me. Gentile and Whitehead are difficult but if I read slowly I understand, but I admit that I do not feel that I understand your brother. When you explained that he considered Ruskin's cat unreal because only Ruskin saw it I understood, and was able to refute his position from my own memory.

Yes, I recognised your hand in that essay, and thank you for your quotation from myself.

[W. B. YEATS : *unsigned*]

80

[*after 23rd June 1926*]

My dear Yeats,[1]

As you say the point is too difficult to discuss in letters and I think it best to leave philosophers out of it. Natural science used to be called natural philosophy, and so, with many others, what is called science now was supposed to come into the field of philosophy, but as proof and counterproof coalesce the branches of knowledge are called science.

With respect to the two pictures on the wall and Ruskin's cat, if there was a cat and two pictures what are we arguing about? The friend of Ruskin saw no cat, only saw Ruskin's action. I understood you to suppose that the friend represented common sense, and that your nearer approach to the wall to correct your double vision did also imply that everybody would have agreed with you about one picture and would mostly not have agreed about the two. If you say that both were either real or not real that is equal—what are we arguing about?

There is a distinction made in language between an illusion and a true perception. You say they are either both illusion or both true perceptions. But you admit that most people are deceived into thinking them different, though they are really the same. But you admit that these most people who are deceived truly exist, because otherwise how do you know what they think. It is therefore in this sense that Ruskin's cat is an illusion, that most people would not have seen it, though they do see and know that class of objects and events included in my brother's

[1] This letter is copied from a page in Sturge Moore's handwriting, undated and unsigned but apparently a draft for an answer to Yeats's letter No. 79 of 23rd June 1926. The letter may not have been sent as it was not with the other letters and as the ideas in the last two paragraphs are repeated in paragraph 3 of his letter No. 83 of about 27th June 1926. The draft is given here on account of the further steps in the discussion revealed in the first two paragraphs.

first proposition. Therefore Ruskin's cat is not one of those things that to deny the truth of is to contradict yourself, and in this it differs from most cats, which if you deny that they are known to exist by other people you contradict yourself because if other people are known to exist most cats are known to exist in the same sense. And Ruskin's cat is not in this position and cannot get into it. It is therefore in a class apart and is distinguished from other cats by not having the characteristics of knowledge, i.e. that the propositions true about things known are not true about it.

You cannot converse without alluding to other people and objects, therefore if you deny the truth of their existence you contradict yourself. If you call all things, including yourself and other selves and all objects, illusion then the meaning of illusion for you is just what others mean by real and the dispute is verbal and an illusion also. There is no difference between you and your fellow-illusions save one of vocabulary.

81

Kildare Street Club, Dublin.

25th June [1926]

My dear Sturge,

I am up in Dublin for a day and have read the essay of your brother's with great care. I understand him now. I certainly mis-understood him and thereby showed myself a very careless and impatient person about 'possibilities' and 'double images.'

My description of him as believing in nothing but sense-data was taken from a description of his belief by some other philo-sopher. It is a fair enough statement if put in the form 'We have direct knowledge of sense-data alone.' This is what I have argued against—at least if sense-data is used in his sense. I will write from Ballylee.

I came to Dublin to get an attack on the King for opening the Tate while the Lane picture matter was *sub judice* into the Dublin

press. I do not know whether I have succeeded or not. If I have
the English press will probably quote. In any case I shall attack
him in the Senate—unless some new fact emerges.

Yours ever

W. B. YEATS

82

82 Merrion Square S. Dublin.

26th June [*1926*]

My dear Sturge,

I have read your brother and am full of surprise. He says in
effect: 'I think that certain popular beliefs are certainly true, that
there are material objects, that the earth existed before there were
ever human beings, that there are space and time—but if you ask
me why I know this I can only say they seem true. I have had
evidence but I have forgotten it. I admit that there are other
popular beliefs which are not true. I do not believe that there is
a God or a soul, for instance. But when you ask me why I reject
some beliefs and accept others I say I do not know. In practice
language gives me a criterion. If a man's word literally understood contradicts his intended meaning that man contradicts himself and the literal meaning of his words is his real belief. Of course
I know this is not always so.' (Your brother has not actually said
this but must mean it.) 'If he says "John Smith has had a stroke"
it does not follow that he believes somebody has knocked John
Smith down. But in some cases (which I select because it seems
to me that it is so in these cases) he does contradict himself.'

This is an expression of faith and arises from a special
experience, just as the saint's and the ascetic's expression of faith
does, just as Nietzsche's does when he says 'Am I a barrel of
memories that I should give you my reasons?' But we cannot
discuss it; we can only accept or reject it.

Interest begins for me when your brother goes on to draw
conclusions which contradict my special experience.

103

(1) He builds up certain reasoning on the fact that if you look at your hand through the naked eye and through a microscope you see different things. He had no right to draw any conclusions about the external world from this without pointing out that it was proved years ago that a vision in a crystal could sometimes be magnified in exactly the same way. An external world can be experimentally created. The hypnotist creates it by suggestion (all suggestion, by the bye, is really in the end autosuggestion) and once created it runs for a certain course of time before the eyes—occasionally of several people, as some know, I know, for instance. All your brother's analysis as it is found in this essay (and in what I read in his *Refutation of Idealism*) can be applied to that experimentally created world.

(2) He says that no physical fact in his belief 'logically' depends upon any mental fact, and seems to have entirely ignored all evidence derived from that experimentally created world and all inference to be drawn from allied psychical evidence of every kind.

(3) He says there is no such thing as 'timeless consciousness' and does not even discuss the evidence for prevision given by people like Richet and Myers. If I can see the future my consciousness is in that degree exempt from a condition of time.

Part of the trouble is that your brother, like the ecclesiastics, does not examine evidence because he is satisfied with faith or thinks evidence is impossible, and another part is that your brother has that English University habit which made it possible for the editors of *The Cambridge Ancient History* to ignore India and China and that keeps all English Universities entirely ignorant of the arts. Shadwell, the translator of Dante, thought Doré's Dante illustrations magnificent works. This is English provincialism. That damned 'silver sea.'

Yours ever

W. B. YEATS

P.S. Here is a very strange thing which will show you what I meant when I wrote of individual man not being shut up in a bottle. I published a few weeks ago a book called *A Vision*. In that there is a summing-up of European history which I divide into certain epochs. I have just got Spengler's *Decline in the West*. I was writing my notes and drawing my historical diagrams in Galway while his first edition was passing through the press in Germany. I had never heard his name, and yet the epochs are the same, the dates are the same, the theory is the same—even some of my examples, such as the drilling of the eye in the Roman statues, and the screwing on of Roman portrait heads to ready-made conventional bodies, and these examples are used to prove the same things. I can almost say of his book and of the historical part of mine that there is no difference in our interpreta-tion of history (an interpretation that had never occurred to any-body before) that is not accounted for by his great and my slight erudition. Get my book from some library—it is too expensive to buy—and above all get his.   W. B. Y.

83*

Last Sunday [*27th June 1926*]

My dear Yeats,

Here is your third letter and I cannot send this today.

There is no doubt that my brother would allow that Ruskin's cat was sense-data for Ruskin and that he had direct knowledge of them though they were absent from among the sense-data of his friends. It is this last fact that differentiates R.'s experience from any ordinary experience.

But it is equally certain that Ruskin's cat was not among the things we know, as defined in my brother's first two propositions, and does involve a contradictory assumption of the truth of two mutually exclusive propositions.

Direct knowledge is neither the only nor a certainly true form of knowledge. We see the sunset and have direct knowledge of a going down but we know the earth moved us behind its rotund contour and that the sun did nothing it is not always doing. We know that certain interpretations of sense-data do not involve self-contradictory propositions while others do. Your interpretation of Ruskin's adventure with the cat does.

June 30th. Here is your fourth letter since one of mine! I think you misunderstand my brother, as I said in a former letter, because you are interested in finding an imagined hypothesis which will reconcile certain strange facts. He, like Newton, starts out by refusing to make hypotheses however strange the facts. He would reply to your assertion that material objects cannot exist, nor space nor time, because of M. Richet's experiments or of Ruskin's cat, etc.: 'Well and good! All that can wait. What do you mean by M. Richet or Ruskin or most people if you don't mean my first two propositions? And if you don't mean them, what are you talking about to me, for I also am in the same class with them? If I do not exist in the sense that supposes my first two propositions to be true neither do you, nor M. Richet, nor Ruskin nor his cat, and we know nothing whatever about them, because what our words about them mean is this that my first two propositions explain. This is what we really all mean by knowing and we cannot assert anything about M. Richet or Ruskin without implying that my first two propositions are true, for if we don't admit their truth we can't help contradicting ourselves, or at least rendering our statement meaningless. Then you ask me how I know that what is true is true; I reply that if my argument is sound, and it seems to me that it is, then it is true. But if it is not sound show me where my argument goes astray.'

What he means, I suppose, by the evidence we once had for the existence of other things before ourselves is what the child in birth must have had if it could have recorded it in memory, or the foetus at any earlier moment before. We have a right to assume we might have had this evidence if we had been able to record it in memory. It is in a sense recorded in our present existence.

He does not assert that there is no God, or no soul, only that as far as he is concerned there is no argument for their existence which he has examined which did not rest on a logical mistake, on using one word in two senses without noticing that one was doing so. Therefore, he says he sees no reason for supposing either to exist.

He is always very willing to admit that all he has done takes us nowhere towards settling the puzzles which interest you, such as how Ruskin came to see and lift a cat that another man near him could not see or hear or touch. Or how anyone could foresee the future, in cases where there is respectable evidence for their having done so. Or how a vision in a crystal could be magnified, if it was. But he asserts that if we want to know what we know we must make no mistakes over deducing what we think from what we thought, or what the words used mean in this case from what they meant in that. And this, he asserts, speculative philosophers have always done and can be proved to have done. But he freely admits that he cannot analyse the implications contained in the assertion that an object *is* or a person *is*.

You are simply not interested in such questions. He refuses to form an opinion on the questions that interest you until he can arrive at them without leaving a mistake or a hiatus in reasoning behind him. And he can't do this yet, so he leaves such questions alone, pending the invention of a sound technique for dealing with them.

There is no question of faith save *that* we all have, namely that we know we are and that other things and persons are, though what is implied in this knowledge has not yet been discovered. It is as modest a creed as well could be, and he tries to show that it is logically unassailable, whereas most philosophers start out by positing something inconsistent with it.

Language makes a distinction between reality and illusion. This distinction may be unanalysable but is none the less a true distinction for all that. Ruskin's cat is not one of those things to deny the truth of the reality of which involves you in a self-contradiction, and in this differs from most cats. If you deny that most cats are known to exist by other people you contradict yourself because if other people are known to exist most cats are in the same sense. But Ruskin's cat is not in this position and cannot get into it. It is therefore in a class apart and may be an illusion. You cannot converse without implying the real existence of other people and other objects, therefore if you deny that they exist you contradict yourself. If you call all things, including yourself, other selves and objects, illusions, then the meaning you give illusion is that which others give to real, and there is no difference between you and your fellow illusions save one of vocabulary. You prefer to call black white whereas they call black black. What we mean by real is that which most cats are and apparently Ruskin's cat was not, i.e. creatures that were once born and have since been always in certain relations to objects on the earth. This is the meaning of real cat or real object.

Yours ever

T. S. MOORE

P.S. Your evidence for the absence of objective reality implies the presence of all that is meant by objective reality, namely that M. Richet, Ruskin and his cat were once born and lived in relations to this earth that were and seemed to them both spatial and temporal. Spatial and temporal relations involve us in some difficulties about observed facts, relativity, the quantum theory. These difficulties are of the same nature that used to be presented by the movements of stars, or were presented by the discovery of radium. But your idea that suggestion can account for them begs the question because suggestion implies the existence of persons and objects to be suggested and to suggest and therefore cannot account for their existence.

84*

Savile Club, 107 Piccadilly, W.1.

23rd May [*1927*]

My dear Sturge Moore,

     I have just seen Macmillan about my new book. It will be

published, as will all my other books until they are ready to be added to the collected edition, in a different form from that of the collected edition. I want you to design the cover—design in gold—and a frontispiece. The book is to be called *The Tower*, as a number of the poems were written at and about Ballylee Castle. The frontispiece I want is a drawing of the castle, something of the nature of a woodcut. If you consent I will send you a bundle of photographs. It is a most impressive building and what I want is an imaginative impression. Do what you like with cloud and bird, day and night, but leave the great walls as they are.

I am here for a few days probably until the beginning of next week. My wife thought me run down or something of the kind and so sent me off to enjoy life, which I am not doing.

Yours ever

W. B. YEATS

85

Hillcroft, Steep, Petersfield, Hampshire.

24th May 1927

My dear Yeats,

I shall be very glad to design a cover and frontispiece for your volume if you will send on the photos, and have the exact measures for the cover sent, and of the square of type so that the frontispiece may be in proportion with the type. A dummy book and a specimen page would be most useful .

We are sorry you are not enjoying life in London and wish we could invite you down to this most enjoyable country and weather but we are just sending Dan off to Australia and shall be seeing him off in London in a day or so. He is going out as an emigrant to try his fortune and his mother is very busy getting his clothes etc. ready and there are a thousand things to see to, so that we can't be as hospitable as we should like.

There is a Blake Exhibition at the Burlington Club got up by Archie Russell. I mention it in case you should not have heard of it. It is said to be very good, and so is the Jewish or Yiddish play *The Dybbuk* at the Royalty.

Yours ever

T. S. MOORE

86*

82 Merrion Square S. Dublin.

[*before 2nd June 1927*]

Dear Sturge Moore,

I have heard from Macmillan today: the new book, *The Tower*, is to be uniform in size with *The Wild Swans at Coole* which you no doubt have. Macmillan has now got the Manuscript and will no doubt begin printing it at once, and is probably therefore in a hurry for the designs.

I have got two fine Japanese Nōh Masks and am trying to get some magnificent masks made by the Dutch Sculptor Van Krop for my *Only Jealousy of Emer*. With these masks I shall be able to give a series of Dance Plays here, as we have just added to the Abbey Theatre a small perfectly equipped theatre which holds a hundred people. I am hoping henceforth with the assistance of the Abbey School of Acting to make experiments for which the popular audience of a larger theatre is not ready. As the Young Players of the school will be comparatively inexperienced there will be some advantage in letting them appear before the public in a strange dramatic form, related rather to ritual than to the ordinary form of drama.

The Abbey itself is prospering to my perpetual astonishment, even increasing its capital. At the moment, however, it is threatened with disaster. Its whole career this winter may depend upon an interview I am to have at two o'clock today with the leading lady who wants to accept an engagement in America to get out of the reach of her family. I have to persuade her to suffer.

Yours ever

W. B. YEATS

87*

82 Merrion Square S. Dublin.

2nd June [1927]

My dear Sturge Moore,

I return the design. It is interesting that you should have completed Tower symbolism by surrounding it with water.

I enclose a photograph of Ballylee, where I return on Friday.

You will have had my letter so I need not again say how admirable the bookplate promises to be.

By the bye, I had a successful performance of my *Only Jealousy of Emer* the other day.

Yours ever

W. B. YEATS

88*

Hillcroft, Steep, Petersfield, Hampshire.

[after 2nd June 1927]

My dear Yeats,

I will put the drawing in hand and submit it again to you before it is cut. Many thanks for all you say about it.

On the philosophical point, you certainly do not understand my brother's position, which is that all philosophers, Plato, Plotinus, Croce, Whitehead, anyone who denies his first two propositions or attempts to explain them away, must always fail to make a positive proposition at variance with them which does not contradict itself. He does adopt the expression 'physical fact' in an ordinary acceptation and therefore does support Bertie Russell against your point (page 208). He does not adopt Mill's expression (permanent possibility) and thinks it is only just possible that its meaning may be true, but is far from believing it true. As far as I can understand your position, it is included among those which he reduces to absurdity between page 200 and page 205 of the *Contemporary British Philosophy*, second series.

It is this preliminary argument which seems to me fatal to all speculative views such as yours. They cannot represent the fact. Any value they may have must be similar to that a work of art has, not similar to a statement of fact.

My brother puts in place of them only and merely his first two propositions, and adds that he has as yet discovered no satisfactory analysis as to what those two true propositions actually imply. He gives three analyses of them that seem possibly true, but adopts neither of them and suggests very real difficulties in the way of the adoption of any one of them.

From my own point of view I prefer the simplest and least imaginary philosophy because I can do the imaginary part myself and find that his two propositions give me all I want, though I should be very glad to have more if more could be proved in the sense that those two propositions are. It also seems to me possible that some day my brother's position may be turned not by philosophy but by science, but this will not alter its impregnability as opposed to the speculative reasoners. It will only give him a fourth and better analysis of the implications of his two propositions. I found this idea on what I have learnt from you or through you about materialisations, with the facts about which my brother has not yet concerned himself.

I am glad to hear of a successful performance of *The Only Jealousy*, which is the one I like best of all your mask plays. I wish we could see it in London.

With many thanks,

Yours sincerely
T. S. MOORE

P.S. Many thanks for the photo of the Tower which is a beautiful building and was not architecturally done justice to in the drawing I saw before.

89*

Thoor Ballylee, Gort, Co. Galway.

15th September [*1927*]

My dear Sturge Moore,

No, I am sorry but I don't like that young woman. The right leg seems thick and clumsy and the head looks immense and is without charm. I sometimes like your figures, but I always like your beasts and your decoration. I like the landscape in this greatly, and am convinced if the dancer were a unicorn or such I would like all. You have had a lot of trouble with the thing and I am remorseful. Perhaps if you put it aside for a few weeks something would suggest itself. I do want something Anne may care for all her life.

I did not go on with correspondence for we had come to an agreement upon essentials. I am now deep in Croce. I have finished his *Philosophy of the Practical*, all of his *Aesthetics* except the historical chapters, which I shall return to, and am half through the *Logic*. I find this kind of study helps my poetry which has I believe been at its best these last few months—indeed I am writing nothing but poetry.

Yours

W. B. YEATS

P.S. What's wrong with Croce is that he knows how the bird gets out of the egg but has no notion how it got in.

90

82 Merrion Square S. Dublin.

21st September [*1927*]

My dear Sturge Moore,

Macmillan has now got all the manuscript for my book and so will I suppose send you in a few days the necessary measurement. I find that the only typed copy of the book as a whole has been sent off, but I am sending you certain poems dealing with

H   113

the Tower as that is your main concern, and I shall add one or two others if I can find copies. I am also sending you some photographs of the Tower. I need not make any suggestions, except that the Tower should not be too unlike the real object, or rather that it should suggest the real object. I like to think of that building as a permanent symbol of my work plainly visible to the passer-by. As you know, all my art theories depend upon just this—rooting of mythology in the earth.

I see that the topic of our late impassioned correspondence, Bertrand Russell, has mended his hand, at least if I can trust that fallacious person Noyes, and declares that a thought and a billiard ball are made of the same 'neutral substance.' Ruskin's cat comes into his own and I now no more denounce Bertrand Russell than I do any other peaky-nosed, bald-pated, pink-eyed harridan. I prefer Swedenborg's muscular angels that move 'towards the day-spring of their youth.'

Yours ever

W. B. YEATS

Instead of sending you typed script I lend you a copy of *October Blast* which makes one section of my new book. I wish I could give it you but it is the only copy I have and the book is out of print.

91*

40 Well Walk, Hampstead, London.

16 November 1923 [*1927*]

Dear Yeats,

I return your photos and book as the cover design is cut. Shannon says you ought to be very pleased as it is both very original and very good. He said he meant to write to you to that effect but I daresay he has not, as he hates writing letters and during Ricketts's absence has a double quantity to answer.

I think that the Tower is recognisably your Tower and not anyone else's.

We are not comfortable yet but hope to be so when the last workman has left and we can begin to live again.

We look forward to your coming to see us whenever you are in London and shall usually be able to put you up, so I hope you will let us know when you are coming.

With best wishes

Yours ever

T. STURGE MOORE

92*

Grand Hotel Madrid, Seville.

18th November [*1927*]

My dear Sturge Moore,

What has happened about the cover design etc.? I have heard nothing, perhaps because some letters have not yet reached me. I have been ill—pneumonia—and have been sent here to make a pleasant, slow and expensive recovery. I have acquired a lung, and walk about in the sun feeling very old and dignified, and look forward to some weeks of the gardens of the Alcazar, dropping crumbs to some equally old and dignified goldfish. But do send me a word.

I am reading that bald-pate daily. When I read him before I knew little, but now for four years I have read nothing but philosophy and I understand what has happened. The scientific and psychological parts are amazingly acute, but as for the philosophy—the bald-pate sprouts radishes.

Yours ever

W. B. YEATS

Have you read Wyndham Lewis's new book? What an entangled Absalom! We have decided to move on to Cannes, as this place does not suit my lung. Write c/o Thomas Cook & Son, Rue Maréchal Foch, Cannes, France.

93

40 Well Walk, Hampstead, London
(at 22 The Spain, Petersfield, till the 29th).

23rd December 1927

My dear Yeats,

I have been meaning to write to you for many weeks, but when your letter arrived I had only recently posted one to you answering all your questions about the cover, which I suppose will have been forwarded to you. And now perhaps you are already back in Dublin? I was very sorry to hear you had been so ill and pneumonia is a nasty thing to have. However I hope you will get completely over it and have no returns or aftermaths.

I have read in Lewis's last book and read all his *Lion and Fox*. As you say, his hair is dangerously long and he is too suspicious all round, but there is something of genius if only he could get and keep hold of it. I am about to start on his *The Wild Body*, a set of tales many of which I read ten years ago with great admiration but he has completely rewritten them. I could not guess who was the 'Bald Pate' you were re-reading as you did not name him.

Ricketts is back from America extremely impressed by their Museums and private collections, the right thing done without any halfheartedness or paltering. He says you find genuine £40,000 Titians and Rembrandts in houses of less appearance than Townsend House, where only one maid is kept, yet they are well hung and well lit and surrounded by a consciousness that the picture gives dignity to the house and no suggestion of a pretence the other way. He evidently wants to go back.

With best wishes for the coming year (we have had the most awful move we have ever made and still have rain through the roof and workmen in and books in a muddle).

Yours ever

T. S. MOORE

94*

Hôtel Château St. Georges, Route de Fréjus, Cannes.

[after 23rd December 1927]

My dear Sturge Moore,

No, I never got that letter which 'answered all questions.' Several letters seem to have gone astray. I know nothing except that Macmillan thinks you 'are satisfied with the cutting' of the block for the cover. Did you do the frontispiece of *The Tower?*

I have had a long illness and my wife thinks I must be prepared for a couple more months of it—bleeding in the lung from blood-pressure, and much exhaustion. In the morning I generally feel quite well and am longing to be at work but the doctor even forbids serious books. I have had to lay aside Hegel, and even Bertrand Russell's last—he now thinks that physical objects are merely appearances and that nothing is real but space-time ('the event' or date and place) and this pleases me because it is in the most exact way the doctrine of ancient astrology. It was never, as modern astrologers think, the 'influence' of this or that star that mattered but always date and place. The stars were figures on a clock-face. However he will be always bald. I prefer Absalom.

I defy the doctor, as I do in writing this letter, by reading daily *Time and Western Man* and *The Art of Being Ruled* and feel that henceforth I need not say splenetic things for all is said. He mixes metaphors in the most preposterous way but he can write; he has intellectual passion, and of that there has been very little these thirty years. His last book is among other things Plotinus or some Buddhist answering the astrologers (the only believers ever persecuted by Buddhists). I do not always hate what he hates and yet I am always glad that he hates. There are always men like that. Schopenhauer can do no wrong in my eyes: I no more quarrel with his errors than I do with a mountain cataract. Error is but the abyss into which he precipitates his truth. The more wide-minded men like the beauty of speed.

Yours ever

W. B. YEATS

Write, for I see nobody and long for news.

95*

40 Well Walk, Hampstead, London.

[*before 29th January 1928*]

My dear Yeats,

I am deeply concerned to learn by your letter that you are by no means so well out of the wood as I had supposed from the first one. I am also very annoyed that my letter re the cover which crossed your previous one to me never found you, especially as I have never heard anything about a frontispiece. Macmillans only asked me to do a cover design, but you seem to refer to a frontispiece as well as intended? Shannon very distinctly approved of the cover, on which your Tower is quite recognisable. With my last letter it now occurs to me that I returned your photo, so that is possibly why it was not re-directed to you, as the cost of postage would have been considerable.

I hope your lung will soon heal completely and you must not run any risks; a long period of physical incapacity or partial incapacity is always very trying when the mind remains as active as ever. I wish I had read so much of Absalom's abundance as you seem to have done, but our life has been an unbelievable series of distracting worries owing to our move and the impossible incapacity of the workmen who did up this house, so that I have read very little and done hardly any work since I finished your cover.

I doubt whether there is any meaning in what you say of Russell's latest opinions. The very idea of appearance is that it is of something which presumably may be known by an infinitude

118

of other appearances. What connects all these appearances together? Why are their repetitions dependent on exact sequences of conditions or the appearances of other things? Russell is wildly speculative, and besides that very passionate and personal. Words don't matter: it is the meaning that matters. To call this or that real is quite arbitrary; the only meaning in real is that certain appearances of the thing so called may be trusted to reappear in a given sequence among the appearances of other things. This dependability is reality. Time and space apply to all appearances without exception so that nothing at all appears without their being implied in the sequence. Therefore they are not appearances in the same sense as those of objects are. They apparently do not merely appear to the self but the self appears in them. What is implied in these facts of experience is not known to Russell or anyone else. And it is no use pretending that what is not known is known because somebody has got excited about the possibility that it might be known or will prove to be this or that when it is known. The fact always remains that it is not known.

I quite agree with what you say about Wyndham Lewis being able to write and possessing intellectual passion. He always seemed to me to be a genius but most unfortunate, almost as horribly unfortunate as Baudelaire shows himself to have been in *Mon cœur mis à nu*. I am looking forward to reading his volume of tales *The Wild Body*, many of which I read ten and more years ago in an earlier form and thought highly of. He has re-written them all and added new ones.

Do you see *The Criterion*? I had a little paper called *Towards Simplicity* in the November number.

I have very little news as I have seen hardly anyone yet, being too much taken up with getting this house into working order. I have written a review of the new books on Blake which, alas, may never come out as it is touch and go whether *The Criterion* continues and depends on their getting some capital put into it. The Frenchman Saurat's book on the relation of Blake to Milton is full of suggestion though he himself has not an interesting mind.

He proves that there is a great deal of correspondence between the myth of Paradise Lost and that of Vala. It looks as if Blake had deliberately intended to go one better than Milton, and as if the scheme of Vala had a consciously intellectual and contrived origin.

I hope that you may soon be feeling able to read and work without running the risk of exhaustion, and that with the early Spring of the South your health will return. We were once at a place called Pardigon, a halt on the P.L.M. between La Croix and Cavalaire, but on the Sud-France local line, which consisted of a single eighteenth-century house with a terraced garden in ruins and a magnificent avenue of mimosa straight down to the sea. It was very quiet and moderate and most beautiful. They have since added a wing bigger than the original house but people who have been there still say it is a delightful and exceptional place. I enclose a card, as I should say it would be much nicer than Cannes.

With best wishes
Yours ever
T. S. MOORE

96

40 Well Walk, Hampstead, London.

29th January 1928

My dear Yeats,

I have since receiving yours read *Time and Western Man* and also heard from W. Lewis. Though he was unable to come here, he writes 'The remarks you detail made to you by Yeats are amusing and gratifying. I am glad too that he likes the book. Please if you see him again, remember me to him—we met at your house, you may remember, many years ago.'

Most of his criticisms of Bergson, Whitehead and Alexander are sound enough. He comes apparently very close to my position, though he seems shaky on one or two fundamentals.

120

But one cannot properly tell before he expounds his own position in the book he is now writing. I doubt if he really thinks Space and Time mere appearances, or if he does, I feel sure he is wrong. They are obviously modes of appearances, conditions of experience. There is no proof of any experience without them. He seems to think that Kant's metaphysics was all rot, as my brother does; that he undid what he had done in that part of his works. He finds my brother's realism very much to his mind but seems to think this can consist with Berkeley's idea about things only existing in mind, in which, if he really thinks this, he is certainly wrong. My brother is adverse to the supposition of a god as baseless; Lewis seems to think this supposition necessary. His idea of God is that he has a composite back, as a fly has a composite eye, so that he can be back to back with every soul and that, he, God, is not pleased with those who try to see him over their shoulders, but prefers those who merely lean against him and take no other notice of him, giving all their attention to the world in front of them. My brother would agree with this practical conclusion, only he has an insensitive back and does not feel God's back behind his.

Hoping that you are making good progress in convalescence.

Yours ever

T. STURGE MOORE

97

Hôtel Château St. Georges, Route de Fréjus, Cannes.

February 2nd [1928]

My dear Sturge Moore,

That sentence of yours about Time, Space and Experience has abolished all the philosophers I have ever read—Plato, St. Thomas, Kant, Hegel, Bergsen, and last and least the Bald One. However that very British brother of yours had already abolished the lot. By the bye, please don't quote him again till you have asked him this question: 'How do you account for the fact that when the Tomb of St. Theresa was opened her body exuded miraculous oil and smelt of violets?' If he cannot account for such primary facts he knows nothing.

I get well very slowly. Influenza, two attacks since Christmas, has delayed things, and I am still confined to bed for most of the day. Over-work of years, the doctor says. I have just read you in *The Criterion* for December with approval.

Yours ever

W. B. YEATS

Mr. Wyndham Lewis on Time and Space (see *Time and Western Man,* page 444) 'Appearances riddled with contradictions.'

98

Hôtel Château St. Georges, Route de Fréjus, Cannes.

February 12th [*1928*]

My dear Sturge Moore,

I am afraid it is too late to do anything now about that frontispiece. Macmillan had agreed to it. I wish I had known in time.

I have read *Time and Western Man* with gratitude, the last chapters again and again. It has given, what I could not, a coherent voice to my hatred. You are wrong to think Lewis attacks the conclusions of men like Alexander and Russell because he thinks them 'uncertain.' He thinks them false. To admit uncertainty into philosophy, necessary uncertainty, would seem to him to wrong the sovereignty of intellect, or worse, to accept the hypocritical humility of the scientific propagandists which is, he declares, their 'cloak for dogma.' He is a Kantian, with some mixture of older thought, Catholic or Greek, and has the vast Kantian argument behind him, the most powerful in philosophy. He considers that both 'space and time are mere

122

appearances,' whereas his opponents think that time is real though space is a construction of the mind.

Yours ever

W. B. YEATS

99

Albergo Rapallo, Rapallo.

February 23rd [*1928*]

My dear Sturge Moore,

Your cover for *The Tower* is a most rich, grave and beautiful design, admirably like the place, and I am all the more grateful because I may see but little of that place henceforth. I shall have to spend my winters here, and what time I can give to Ireland in Dublin to oversee the Abbey and see my friends. No, it is not pneumonia that has knocked me out: that only began the business, and though it has left a lung slightly touched, my ailment is over-work. I have been very near a complete breakdown from the over-work of years. The doctors tell my wife that I must withdraw from public life and live far from crowded places, and one of them tells me that I must walk slowly and even move my head slowly that my thought may become slow also. The same man, who until he went into semi-retirement at Monte Carlo was making £30,000 a year in Canada, added 'If I had met you when this was beginning, four years ago, I could have saved you it all by sending you off on a bout of dissipation—all the great creators of the past were devils. Drink and women have saved many a man from death or madness.'

You say again that philosophy is dependent upon science. This opinion prevailed over most of Europe from the time of Mill to the closing years of Herbert Spencer. It prevails nowhere now except in America and among perhaps three of the six-and-thirty British writers on philosophy. Read Croce on the subject in *Aesthetics*. Why should you get caught in the scientific mouse-trap, which is baited with British sentimentality?

123

You say Bertrand Russell says that Kant smashed his own philosophy by his doctrine of practical reason. So he does say, and what more can you expect from a man who has been entirely bald during the whole course of his life. He merely repeats a piece of common electioneering nonsense which writer has copied from writer for generations. The men who invented it had as much to do with philosophy as an Orange brass band on the twelfth of July has to do with religion.

From Buddha's time there have always been the two paths to reality, that of knowledge and that of will. (Zen Buddhism, like Blake and Kant, thought the path of knowledge was closed, that of will open.) St. Paul's Christianity set up the path of will as against the quick path of knowledge; and from Kant have descended two great streams of thought, the philosophy of will in Schopenhauer, Hartmann, Bergsen, James, and that of knowledge in Hegel, Croce, Gentile, Bradley and the like.

The trouble with you is that you take after Bertrand Russell, of whom Lord Haldane said to me 'He has not read philosophy.' Then again, you say of Berkeley's doctrine that 'it is certainly false.' When some time ago I asked you where you got the certainty you referred me to Bertrand Russell's little book in 'The Home Library.' But Bertrand Russell has changed his mind, and in his last book, *An Outline of Philosophy*, on page 301, he 'is not sure' that pure Berkeleianism is wrong. 'We shall therefore' he says 'be prudent if we regard the non-mental events of physics as mere auxiliary concepts, not assumed to have reality but only assumed to simplify the laws of concepts.[1] Thus matter will be a construction built out of percepts, and our metaphysic will be eventually that of Berkeley.' Again and again he insists that, whether we believe in 'non-mental events' or no, if we see a star or examine (to give his instance) what seems another living brain—fitting instruments being granted—all that we see is in our own heads. He himself prefers a less prudent view of the

---

[1] 'Concepts' here is a slip for 'percepts.' Russell in fact goes on to say that in spite of the logical merits of this view he cannot bring himself to accept it.

Sturge Moore's design for the cover of *The Tower*

'non-mental events' as 'intervals' between 'points,' both points and intervals being neither in time nor space, in mind nor body. That is to say time, space, mind and body, when considered in relation to the events, are 'emergent.'

He is evidently full of doubt for he now insists (he took a different view in his early work) that all mathematics are deduced empirically from the 'percepts,' and it certainly is difficult to turn a part of experience into 'a thing in itself' and so put it outside all experience. But then one has to remember that his person is contorted, and all of him an outward expression of essential vacuity and disorder. Having declared that 'events' are neither in mind nor body, time nor space, he proceeds to describe them in words taken entirely from matter and space and calls them 'neutral stuff,' 'wave-lengths,' and so on. He like all of his sort is afraid that if he used any other language he might have to go to Church. He has got the Archbishop of Canterbury in his belly.

This is a plague of a letter, but it is the first long letter I have written since my illness, and I am very puffed up about it.

Yours ever

W. B. YEATS

100

40 Well Walk, Hampstead, London.

1st March 1928

My dear Yeats,

I was very sorry to learn that you have the prospect of a valetudinarian existence before you. But you must not be too resigned to it for Binyon tells me his brother was told just the same thing about its being dangerous to walk except slowly or brusquely move his arm, and that just when he was resigned to those limitations another specialist said that his heart was quite right and it was his appendix or something of the sort which was causing the trouble, and he had an operation and was soon recovered and as hearty as he had ever been. The science of doctors is yet in a very nebulous state and few indeed possess it and at the same time a native flair for the insides of patients. I must say I suspect your doctor's rather melodramatic diagnosis and remedy which it is too late to apply. I should be determined to consult another on the first opportunity.

I am glad you like the cover. I think it looks very well but it would look still better on white vellum if there ever was an opportunity for an *édition de luxe*.

As for philosophy, I have no time to read the long books. I have read Croce's *Aesthetics* in translation and am convinced it is all wrong, just the fashionable impressionism given an air of Hegelianism, and beneath contempt as logic. Heine says that Hegel resembled nothing so much as a mouldy old hen clucking over her mangy chick (his disciples). He had seen and heard the great man, and I feel his judgement would have seemed to me too the correct one. Aldous Huxley in his *Proper Studies* gives some account of Hegel's preposterous presumption in assertion although his statements immediately afterwards were contradicted by new discoveries. And my brother assures me that if you begin at the beginning of these speculative philosophers you almost at once catch them using a word in two quite different senses without noticing what they are doing, with the result that the whole system stands on a simple *non sequitur*.

My view is far from being the old-fashioned materialism of Spencer etc., nor is it the black agnosticism of Anatole France. I saw twenty and more years ago that the discovery of radium knocked the bottom out of these positions. But I do seem to see that all the new discoveries tend to prove that we have no kind of idea of the absolute reality either of thought or matter. The meaning of both words implies an 'of.' A thought of something, about something, may be true or false but it cannot *be* at all without being *of* something which is not part of that thought, and matter is an infinite concord of appearances *of* something which is not an appearance, and while this is the utmost meaning of the words we cannot pretend either to describe reality in the sense in which our experience is real.

Experience is more real than either thought or matter. It is firsthand: they both are deductions from implications of experience. Of course enquiry and will and taste are necessary disciplines, corresponding to their goals, the true, the good and the beautiful, and the supremest poise of art or life implies that all three are harmonized. No one-thing-necessary man can be other than a sectary. Schopenhauer was a kind of Calvinist. He had not the great balanced humanity in which all three disciplines are attuned together. Modern aesthetes, Cézannists, Crocists, etc. are all a lot of puritan sects, one-thing or a-half-thing-necessary men.

Your poems in *The Tower* have a more ample humanity than any of these philosophers could compass, each line appears to you in relation to more kinds of excellence than they ever dreamed of relating their systems to. I greatly admire many of these new poems, especially the first *Meditation in Time of Civil War* and No. 5 of *1919*, *Youth and Age*, the *Two Songs from a Play*, *Colonus' Praise*, and *From 'Œdipus at Colonus'*, and *The Gift of Harun-Al-Rashid*: not that I don't like most of the others too.

Whether there is a supreme mystic experience may be doubted but at any rate no one that claims to have experienced it has been able to say anything significant about it. If it is, it surpasses language, just as philosophy is never equal to language, always being more clumsy than poetry and imagination.

My *Towards Simplicity* was in the November *Criterion*; it was only a review of a stupid Flaubert book which I had in the December number. I heard T. S. Eliot compare Tennyson and Whitman this afternoon. Very acute and quite sound as far as he went, but he evidently does not appreciate good Tennyson more than bad.

With best wishes

Yours ever

T. S. MOORE

101*

82 Merrion Square S. Dublin.

May 29th [1928]

My dear Sturge Moore,

How about the bookplate and the other thing, or did you [not] get my letter?

I think I devined you in the admirable Rossetti essay in the *Supplement* a couple of weeks ago.

Yours

W. B. YEATS

I expect to be in London next month. We could talk things over then.

102

40 Well Walk, Hampstead, London.

31st May 1928

My dear Yeats,

I did not get the letter to which you seem to refer and know nothing about any bookplate.

Yes, the Rossetti essay was mine, slightly reduced on account of length. Glad you liked it.

We shall be delighted to see you when you come to London.

We saw Masefield's Canterbury Mystery the day before yesterday. A most successful performance, but Masefield was perfectly obstinate about letting Ricketts group his players so that R. refused to be present at any performance and only saw the dress rehearsal. The speaking of the verse was not good but the singing was most effective, and so were the costumes in that setting in spite of M. having no idea of grouping them other than that of a sergeant putting them up in a row. R. had been allowed to group the male chorus, which everybody thought the best thing. But everybody was delighted and the text is better than one would

have expected; the press is unanimous in praise, and R. comes in
for his share. Possibly all the other Cathedrals will be wanting
Mystery plays now. There seems to have been no effective
protest yet on the part of the pious.[1]

Hoping that you are feeling better and stronger and that all
your family is well.

Yours ever

T. STURGE MOORE

103*

40 Well Walk, Hampstead, London.

[June 1928]

My dear Yeats,

I enclose a copy of my adaptation of Mallarmé's *Cygne*, page
124 of the ordinary edition of his *Poésies*.

I very much enjoyed seeing you again. My point was that it
is the mechanism of expression which causes the antithesis or
antinomy between *the one* and *the many*. Experience or our senses
and emotions never set before us *the one* or render us conscious of
it. We feel ourselves to be *one among many*, never *to be all in one*.
Thought itself cannot think '*the one*' or '*all in one*,' only language

---

[1] Mr. Masefield's *The Coming of Christ*, with music by Gustav Holst, was
acted in Canterbury Cathedral on 28th and 29th May 1928. The three beautiful
photographs in *The Times* of 28th May 1928, and the same paper's statement
that 'throughout Mr. Ricketts was in the happiest of moods and the mystery
was a memorable pictorial achievement' suggest that a minor theatrical crisis
became somewhat enlarged in the telling. No doubt Ricketts, who was a
perfectionist and accustomed to working with the most graceful and clever
professional actors and actresses of the time, found amateurs difficult to deal
with, specially when, as in this play, they were worried by the costumes, the
acoustics and the fear of turning their backs on the Altar. Perhaps Mr.
Masefield sympathised with them too much to please Ricketts. At all events
those who saw the play agree with Sturge Moore that it was an impressive
performance.

by its mechanism forces this idea before the mind which, though it may be true, we can have no reason, or necessity either, to accept or to reject.

Yours ever

T. STURGE MOORE

104*

Savile Club, 69, Brook Street, W.1

[*June 1928*]

My dear Sturge,

You say 'experience or our senses and emotions never set before us the one or render us conscious of it.' You mean either that 'regularity,' 'universality,' 'unity' are mere names and classifications (Berkeley), or that they are *a priori* forms or rules of the mind which only come into 'existence' through experience (Kant). Coleridge re-stated Kant in terms of Plato and argued that they were 'constitutive' not merely 'regulative,' and he would be supported by various Platonists today. The mind is its own object and sees itself as the necessary truths. The mathematical scientists who say that all must vanish except a mathematic consciousness must think so too. If Kant is right the antinomy is in our method of reasoning; but if the Platonists are right may one not think that the antinomy is itself 'constitutive,' that the consciousness by which we know ourselves and exist is itself irrational? I do not yet put this forward as certainly the thought of my instructors, but at present it seems the natural interpretation of their symbols. I shall wait at least twelve months before I publish. What is the sphere? What are the gyres? Antiquity had both symbols. Is Satan truly an archangel?

The poem is difficult and I hate that shifting of the metaphor from swan to yacht. Does 'low valuing' mean 'low valued' or 'of low value'? Should 'scorn stiffens dream' be 'scorn stiffened dream'? But no, I see that 'the low-valuing spaces' hide snow

131

which swan turns into ice. The dream 'hood-winked' the swan with tedium and then came scorn and its ice. But it is a devilish mixture.

Yours ever

W. B. YEATS

105*

82 Merrion Square S. Dublin.

6th July [*1928*]

My dear Sturge Moore,

I remembered when I got back that when I sign a book for anybody I put a line of verse, very commonly 'For wisdom is a butterfly and not a gloomy bird of prey.' I used to write, in cheerful youth, 'As to living our servants will do that for us.'

Can you leave me space on that design for such a line? I can write quite small if need be. As I grow older I shall probably, as my father did, write smaller and smaller. However if I write too small people will not think they are GETTING GOOD VALUE.

Yours ever

W. B. YEATS

106

c/o Miss Moore, Flora Villa, Cleveland Road, Torquay.

[*after 6th July 1928*]

My dear Yeats,

I seem to have come here without your last letter, so must address through Macmillans. I enclose a rough of the proposed label for signature. I could not remember the exact wording of your quotation but it is of course of no importance; there is room for you to write a considerably longer one. I see how to improve the proportions slightly yet, but the difference would hardly be noticeable to any but professional eyes. This gives the proposed general effect well enough. The wood block will print much clearer: this is a rough pull and smudged. You can have a zinc block made from the drawing which I will do when you send me back this rough; or you can have a zinc block for the lines alone, and the wood block printed through them, which will cost a few shillings more. I expect Emery Walker had better do it in either case.

Hoping you are well
Yours ever
T. S. MOORE

107

Brook Lawn, Howth, Co. Dublin.

[*before 6th September 1928*]

My dear Sturge,

I like the little design very much. I suggest that you either re-draw the little design so that all may be made into a zinc block or that you cut a wood block with lines into which the little wood block would fit. Would not either of these be better than mixing the two kinds of blocks? Yes, Emery Walker should do it.

I shall be here for a month or so. Then back in Dublin at 42 Fitzwilliam Square for another month at any rate. George is in Dublin changing furniture, some of it to Fitzwilliam Square and some to Rapallo—or rather to preliminary storage. I am idle, after living for many busy days in Dublin, partly busy laying plans to fight, or at any rate protest, against the Censorship Bill Holy Church has forced upon the politicians. One cannot be at peace in a country that is half-made unless it is somebody else's country.

Yours ever
W. B. YEATS

133

108

40 Well Walk, Hampstead, London.

6th September 1928

My dear Yeats,

I enclose a proof of the label, which I hope you will like. I think it looks very well. Emery Walker wants to know whether you would like this paper; if you sign the proof you can judge how it feels to write on. Would you like the backs gummed already? If you think of using paste you might just try how this behaves when pasted, as if it cockles easily that would be a reason for choosing another paper. You will see that I have [made] the little block much cleaner and clearer.

We were delighted to read the interview with you about the Censorship Bill and thought it extremely cogent and were sorry to learn that it had not sufficed to prevent that piece of folly.

Hoping that you and all yours are well,

Yours ever

T. S. MOORE

109*

42 Fitzwilliam Square, Dublin.

[after 6th September 1928]

My dear Sturge Moore,

The design is admirable, but if you will try it in a volume of my Collected Edition—have you one? if not I will send one—you will find it is a little too wide. To avoid going across Ricketts's unicorn it will I hope be stuck on top of the bare sheet that faces the unicorn. I think if we leave it as it is it will be clipped. If it is a wood block there is nothing more to be done but if it is a process block of some sort I will not be stone broke if you get Walker to make a smaller block. There would be no harm in having two sizes. Please let me know about this.

The Censorship controversy is lively here. I judge from the

number of anonymous letters I receive that the Catholic press is denouncing me. I don't expect to win because the Republicans, who would like to exclude all English culture, will if they can make the bill even worse. The bill is the result of a propaganda carried on by the Catholic Truth Society and the tourist agent who manages our annual pilgrimage to Lourdes.

Yours ever

W. B. YEATS

110

40 Well Walk, Hampstead, London.

16th September 1928

My dear Yeats,

Emery Walker made the frame larger by a quarter of an inch than my design, for I had measured it exactly to fit a page of your Collected Edition. He found that the block was so much wider than my design that he could not put the framing lines as close as I had indicated, and so set them wider apart, upsetting my proportions slightly. He ought to have let me know before doing this, and I should have told him to send the block round the corner to Lawrence in Red Lion Court that the unnecessary wood might be shaved away. I had at first felt inclined to refuse his block because it does not improve my design but makes the proportions less definite, but Sybil Pye advised me not to trouble about it as no one but me would notice or care. Now I feel inclined to say that it must be done again on account of the difficulty you point out.

Of course it need not be pasted on the page facing Ricketts's Unicorn: in fact I myself should paste it on the next fly-leaf. It also might be pasted in the other way up, as I thought would be done in the case of smaller books. I dont think a reduction would look so well. Perhaps you would let me know whether you would prefer it done again or think it will do pasted sideways on the inner flyleaf? Then I will write or see Emery Walker about it.

He is very anxious that you should not decide to have it printed on gummed paper, as it would print less well on such paper, and points out that it is not you but the people you send it to who will have to mess about with the paste. I dont think it can be clipped: in fact the proof I sent you, owing to my cutting it out in a hurry, has a clipped appearance but of course the real thing will be cut by machinery to the right size, and then any clipping will upset the proportions and spoil the effect. So it must either be done again, which will cost more, though E. Walker ought to stand the racket (still it will be rather hard on him to ask him to), or it must be reduced, which will also cost more and not look so well. Or, it must be pasted in sideways on the second flyleaf where it will not immediately contradict the effect of the upright Unicorn, and look fairly all right though not quite all it should look.

I hope the 'Censor Bill' will be defeated. I had understood from the papers here that it had been passed and was already law.

I am sorry to have been so long-winded but it is difficult to put all the pros and cons of such a thing before anyone by letter.

Hoping that you still keep well as also your wife and children.

Yours ever

T. S. MOORE

III

42 Fitzwilliam Square, Dublin.

23rd September [*1928*]

My dear Sturge Moore,

I wish you would ask Emery Walker what he would charge for a smaller block. A small process block would not cost much. I would hate the idea of anybody putting the label sideways, besides the people I send it to would I am quite certain clip it. There is an experiment I am anxious to make when I get a paste pot. If I damp a label and paste it in the usual way on (say) the second leaf, will it crumple up the page? I put my bookplates on the first or second leaf of some books George and I own in common (Morris's Collected Edition), because her bookplate was on the inside of the cover, and they crumpled up the page in a most damnable way. I think that will always happen if one damps the paper. Is that an argument in favour of gum and a lick, or in favour of a certain kind of paper, or of paste and no damping of page beforehand (which one's correspondents may not understand)? Of course all my books will not have the Unicorn but I have to think of those that have.

I am still working at the Censorship quarrel. My interview in *The Manchester Guardian* started it off. The *Irish Statesman* and *Irish Times* have kept it going. I will send you an *Irish Statesman* with a letter of mine intended to draw the Catholic theologians. We are having a great effect on the intelligentsia but whether we reach the politicians (now all on holiday) I do not know.

Yours ever
W. B. YEATS

I have just looked again at the Collected Edition of Morris. A few volumes are spoilt by the first leaf being crumpled; then I see we stopped in despair. I have found one volume in which George defied precedent and put on her bookplate—mine was inside cover—without first damping it and the page hardly crumpled at all. That it is very slightly crumpled is perhaps an argument for gum, as paste must always damp the paper more than gum. I could have both gummed and not gummed labels. One would only want gum when book contains Unicorn. What do you think?

112

40 Well Walk, Hampstead, London.

25th September 1928

Dear Yeats,

I will ask Emery Walker re the smaller block and about pasting in. I believe there is what is called 'Photo-mount,' a kind of paste with next to no moisture in it, which almost entirely obviates the difficulty about cockling the paper. It is like jelly. I do not think that even the smaller block can look presentable on the same page as Ricketts's Unicorn. Even face to face with it it would not look well. So if you object to putting it on a blank face the only way will be to have the small block printed on a piece of paper large enough to completely hide the end paper design, which is no doubt what most collectors would do. Ricketts's design will appear at the other end of the book. I fear what you say, that the owners of the book would certainly clip the design, is good ground for having a small version that will go across the width. I am putting all these points to E. Walker.

I look forward to reading your letter to *The Irish Statesman*; it has not yet arrived. But many thanks for sending it. Wyndham Lewis says you have made some very interesting comments on his *Childermas*. It is a most interesting performance, more like Rabelais (only most unhappy) than anything else.

I expect gummed labels would require much more moisture than good photomount.

Yours ever

T. S. MOORE

113

42 Fitzwilliam Square, Dublin.

26th September [*1928*]

My dear Sturge Moore,

I have been waiting to send you my *Spectator* and *Irish Statesman* articles together. It is a question of one journey not two to get copies.

I think some prints on a sheet of paper large enough to block out the Unicorn might be the best way, if I had some on small pieces of paper also. I have put the one copy you sent me, after pasting but not otherwise wetting it, on the second page of one

of my books but found I had to clip it. It has cockled very slightly.
I think however that no piece of paper will lie flat unless first
damped or very thin—newspaper cuttings lie flat. I notice that
the small piece of paper with your design shows that it is not the
same kind of paper as the black paper I have put it on and that
this does not look quite right. I suggest a slightly brown paper
which would be a contrast—such a paper as Craig uses—and that
I be given two sizes, one quite small and one to cover the Unicorn
page.

Yours ever

W. B. YEATS

114

40 Well Walk, Hampstead, London.

4th October 1928

My dear Yeats,

Many thanks for *The Spectator* and cutting from *The Irish Times*.
I read your article with admiration: it is splendidly written and
absolutely convincing. I will show both to W. Lewis next
Tuesday. Would you like me to return them after that, as you
might like to send them to someone else?

I went to Emery Walker and saw a very nice man who said
the block should be done again, and that you can have some on
paper the size of the inside of the cover for pasting into the
Collected Edition, of which I took him one volume, and some on
paper the size indicated by the design for a label. He seemed to
think it might be difficult to obtain a small quantity of Craig's
paper, and I do not imagine a brownish paper would look well.
But if the complete inside of the front cover is covered there will
be no difficulty about two qualities of paper being pasted together.
He wants to know how many you will want of each, those on
the large paper and the label. But proofs will be sent you first
so you need not make your mind up till then.

I think all the difficulties are now met without extra expense, and hope the next proofs will be wholly satisfactory.

Yours ever

T. STURGE MOORE

115

40 Well Walk, Hampstead, London.

20th November 1928

Dear Yeats,

I ought to have sent you this proof beforehand but I had no address and have only now received it from Wyndham Lewis. This is to paste right over the Ricketts end paper in the Collected Edition. The other size would be just the design cut out close to the end of the lines for non-collected edition volumes. Am I to order one hundred of each?

Hoping that you had a good journey out and are feeling fit for the winter.

Yours ever

T. STURGE MOORE

116*

Via Americhe 12-8, Rapallo.

December [1928]

My dear Sturge Moore,

Many thanks for the labels. I return those for your wife and would have sent them before but for the difficulty of getting a large envelope for them when I dont know a word of the language. I have constantly forgotten to ask my wife to get one.

Our new coinage is going the general round of our Irish enterprises. There has been a public meeting with a Monsignor in the Chair to denounce 'the pagan coinage,' and one of my colleagues has been getting 'a batch of anonymous letters' reproaching him for having allowed his 'Catholic principles' to be 'perverted by the dominating personality of Senator Yeats'— what flattery!—while a priest has written to the press to say it is all the work of Freemasons and is the first step to deprive the Irish people of every trace of religion. They would have been quite happy if we had on the larger coin a cross wreathed in shamrocks.

How much do I owe you for the labels?

Yours ever

W. B. YEATS

117*

Via Americhe 12-8, Rapallo.

[*end of January 1929*]

My dear Sturge Moore,

Did you get a letter I wrote you a good many weeks ago asking what I owed you for those labels? I sent the labels you asked for.

After some cold days I am out on my balcony writing without hat or coat, finding it warmer than indoors.

For my first weeks here I read nothing but Swift but he became too exciting for my blood pressure and so after some sleeplessness I took, on my wife's advice, to detective stories again. Swift's *Epitaph* and Berkeley's *Commonplace Book* are the greatest works of modern Ireland.

Yours ever

W. B. YEATS

118*

40 Well Walk, Hampstead, London.

[*about 1st February 1929*]

My dear Yeats,

I have meant to write to thank you for the label and your letter over and over again, but was always stopped by not knowing what to charge. By the same post with your letter came Emery

Walker's. He charges £2.1.9. for the printing. Perhaps I may charge twice as much for the block etc. though this £4.4.0. seems to make the whole, £6.5.9. rather a lot. If you think it too much please knock some off.

I don't know Swift's *Epitaph* and must look it up. I am sorry you have to be careful, even over reading what interests you supremely. I have by this post sent you a number of *Life and Letters* containing a dialogue written by myself which I hope will amuse you.

I wish we could have a little of your sun. The last few days have been dark and dismal. Have you heard that Shannon, over three weeks ago, fell while hanging a picture on the stairs and hit his head against the marble flags in their hall, and has been unconscious ever since? About a fortnight back Ricketts had given up hope, but Shannon has made steady progress since: takes food well, pulse good, temperature, bones, eyes, everything all right. He mutters and even answers but recognises no one yet. The Doctor expects it will be weeks yet before his memory returns. Ricketts never went to bed for more than a week; then the Doctor gave him a draught and he slept twelve hours on end. He says he dreads letters of sympathy more than anything. But as Shannon's condition daily improves perhaps this will not be so much the case.

Hoping that you and all yours are as well and happy as can be expected, with best wishes for more sun,

Yours ever

T. S. MOORE

119*

Via Americhe 12-8, Rapallo.

24th February [*1929*]

My dear Sturge Moore,

I enclose cheque; the amount is quite moderate, not at all 'a lot.' I should have written before but the cold caught us here and sent me to bed with a rheumatic attack. Now it is warm and my desk does not seem so far off in an uninhabitable climate. For the same reason that I did not write to you I did not write to Ricketts, and now I cannot do so until I know what has happened since you last wrote. I would be greatly obliged if you would write me a short note on the subject when you get this.

I have read you in *Life and Letters* and found much that amused or interested, but I like your dialogues best when they are more philosophical. You defined beauty in a dialogue some years ago in sentences that have become a permanent part of my own view of the world.

I am writing lyrics and have done one I like better than any I have done for some years.

Yours ever

W. B. YEATS

120

40 Well Walk, Hampstead, London.

1st March 1929

Dear Yeats,

Many thanks for your letter and the cheque for £6.5.9. which it contained.

Shannon continues very much the same. I gather that he gets up and can do most things for himself and sometimes seems almost himself even in Ricketts's eyes, though only for a few minutes together; then he loses control of his faculties and becomes irrelevant or fails to direct his hand as he evidently wants to.

Ricketts is very nervous and overworn by the long strain and throws too much imagination into hope but above all into depression, and is often convinced that Shannon will never be himself again, though the doctors say there is very good hope that he may. R. accuses them of lying etc. etc.

I met Dulac there last week and R. seemed to find real relief in talking to him; his Latin mind seemed to make the right remarks.

I am sorry to hear you have had a bad turn of rheumatics, and hope you have not got a return of cold weather as we have here. I am glad my Dialogues amused and interested you. I am hoping to do two or three others, which will gradually bring out the more philosophical sides of the ideas suggested. I wish you would quote me my definition of beauty because I am unable to be sure to what you refer.

I see that the Irish Government has had to accept one radical amendment of the Censor Bill, and may possibly have to accept others.

Our love and best wishes to you and all yours,

T. STURGE MOORE

121*

Via Americhe 12-8, Rapallo.

9th March [*1929*]

My dear Sturge Moore,

Your definition of beauty was 'the body as it can be imagined as existing in ideal conditions' or some such phrase. I understand it as including all the natural expressions of such a body, its instincts, emotions, etc. Its value is in part that it excludes all that larger modern use of the word and compels us to find another word for the beauty of a mathematic problem or a Cubist picture or of *Mr. Prufrock*. It does not define ideal conditions nor should it do so, and so it remains a starting point for meditation. I have written seven poems since February 6th, when I began to write verse again after a year and a half almost of stoppage and find myself very abundant. This undistracted life suits me and

I dread the return in the first days of May to my torpedo fish of a country.

Yours ever

W. B. YEATS

122*

Via Americhe 12-8, Rapallo.

24th March 1929

My dear Sturge,

Why do you embarrass your admirers by wrapping your book in a skittish work of art? What are they to do with it? Are they to clip it out and stick it inside one of the covers? Or put it in the wastepaper basket to corrupt the housemaid? Recover from this accursed habit of the publishers and plant the next design on the cover. I am reading your book in bed in the mornings and finding it full of wisdom, but why do you first dismiss Platonic ideas as phantoms and then go on to accept them and describe them exactly as Plotinus does? They are to him the 'prior' of all experience, and that line and a half of verse you quote is their perfect definition. You may be right in dismissing Cézanne and his school as showing the corrupting influence of science upon art, and yet you cling to a form of philosophy similarly corrupted. You quote Professor Taylor admirably and approvingly but you should get his two great books on Plato, for they are the reasoning behind the very passage which you have quoted. I am delighted with the affectionate way in which you handle Alexander—'This worthy father of a family whom I am kicking on the shins, this benefactor of the whole human race whose jaw I am about to smash.' I only wish that you would go on to express your admiration for the rest of his school in the same way.

Your book is difficult reading, though I dont complain of that, and it will be some time before I have really mastered it. I shall either write again about it or see you in London. I shall be there on the 1st of May if a dance play of mine does not come off in Dublin on the 29th of April, and if it does at some later date. The dance play is a new version of my *Only Jealousy [of Emer]* arranged for the ordinary stage and with much more dancing. George Antheil is writing the music: his music for *Oedipus* has been a great success in Vienna. If I knew one tune from another I should probably hate it for I judge from Ezra's conversation that his affinities are all with the youngest of the young. Not knowing anything about music, however, I am delighted to find a man whose theories about the relations between words and music seem to be exactly my own. In my moments of personal hopefulness—Edwin Ellis's definition of vanity—I begin to think that what my friends call my lack of ear is but an instinct for the music of the twelfth century.

I suppose your Professor Taylor is the author of the two works on Plato. One of these, the longest, on the *Timaeus*, I have in Dublin. I had been reading them for a couple of months when I left. I brought no works of philosophy here as I had to get back to pure literature.

One sentence of yours I hoot at. You have taken it from some rascally philosopher science has corrupted and who, as Blake charged against his predecessors, insists on mystery, as the priests do, to enslave his betters. Hegel set free the human soul when he declared ('the thing is itself,' this theological echo had just been proved unnecessary) that 'there is nothing that is not accessible to intellect.' One must qualify this sentence but it still keeps sufficient truth. Your sentence dismisses the great philosophical systems, as the priests do, as works of imagination, and yet the logic of Kant and that built upon his conclusions cannot be so dismissed, unless it be first disproved, and that seems to me beyond us both. If one assumes, as I think you told me your brother did, (it is certainly necessary if we are to avoid the opinion rejected by Taylor in your extract) that mind and matter are one in a 'prior' state, mind has still its secret entrance there. That still seems to me often bounded on the one side by waking and on the other

by falling asleep. All that I know of any value has come from sleep
—or, to put it otherwise, bounded by dying or being born.

Yours ever

W. B. YEATS

123*

Via Americhe 12-8, Rapallo.

28th March [*1929*]

My dear Moore,

I am still driving my plough into your rich soil. As I read on my
first thoughts prove misunderstandings and I think I shall be in
entire agreement in the end. There are four lines of Swift that I
find good guides, if one substitutes 'percept' for 'matter' and
'intellect' for 'form'—though that is to modernise, not to
improve:—

> *Matter as wise logicians say*
> *Cannot without a form subsist;*
> *And form, say I as well as they,*
> *Must fail, if matter brings no grist.*

When I wrote you first I thought you more subjected than
you are to the rat-catchers and cockle-pickers, who would deny
us the right to draw conclusions from those experiences common
to all men before they have caught the last rat and picked the
last cockle. I do not think your Taylor can be the Platonist for I
cannot imagine A. E. Taylor spending 400 pages among them.

I begin each day—I must stay in bed till 11.30—with Spengler
volume II, and then take up your book. Lunch over, I should
write verse or prepare for it. It will be some time therefore before
I have mastered you.

Yours ever

W. B. YEATS

124*

40 Well Walk, Hampstead, London.

[*after 28th March 1929*]

My dear Yeats,

I was delighted to get your two letters and to find that my book was interesting you in so lively a manner. I had been told that Ricketts had told Lowinski that he agreed with every word of it and indeed 'might have written it himself!' When he spoke to me himself he mixed a good deal of water into this heady wine.

Have you received his splendid Dialogue yet? It is a most beautiful book, beautifully written. Perhaps he is waiting to give you a copy himself. I know he intended you to have one.

There are no approvals that I more desire and prize than yours and his, so that I am considerably elated.

What a pity that Richmond confided my book to the writer of the wishy-washy palaver that appears on the front page of the *Literary Supplement* with several drops of malignity in the mush.

I hope I shall see you at the end of the month when you pass through town. I am not sure that Swift's 'form' is the equivalent of my 'intellect.' Intellect in my view deals with the abstract relations between forms by which appearances are perceived; therefore forms can have aesthetic value which intellects cannot have.

I believe my Taylor is Dr. A. E. Taylor and your Platonist. His was only one of a number of essays dealing with evolution: he dealt with evolution as related to philosophy. His essay was perhaps fifty pages long; nowhere near four hundred. I met him in Scotland at St. Andrews. I think Wyndham Lewis is quite right in thinking Spengler worthless, though I have not read him, but no one takes him seriously I find.

We have had a return of winter after some premature summer days.

Hoping to see you shortly and to hear that we are in the

essential agreement that you look forward to finding between
us when you have read me to the end.

Yours ever

T. S. MOORE

125*

Via Americhe 12-8, Rapallo.

9th April [*1929*]

My dear Sturge Moore,

I enclose an extract from a Dublin newspaper which puts
plainly the difference between your philosophy and mine. It
was written by Judge Meredith, who seems to be re-translating
all Kant's works. He astonished me some years ago (I doubt if I
had even met him) by dedicating his first translation to me. I
think it is a vain hope that I shall some day master it. It was
Kant's *Aesthetics.*

The book reviewed is by Macran, who blossoms (in spite of
much intoxication) admired by all in the free eighteenth century
air of Dublin University. A few years ago a friend of mine saw
him being bundled late at night into a cab by a firm waiter. As
the cab drove off Macran put his head out of the window to
shout: 'Closing Time—time—time. What's time? Time is the
moving shadow of Eternity.'

I feel that an imaginative writer whose work draws him to
philosophy must attach himself to some great historic school.
My dreams and much psychic phenomena force me into a certain
little-trodden way but I must not go too far from the main
European track, which means in practice that I turn away from
all attempts to make philosophy support science by starting with
some form of 'fact' or 'datum': that way lie those deep-sea fish
Taylor objects to in the extract and all the obscurantism of the
Ratcatchers.

Swift's 'form' and 'matter' are 'concept' and 'matter' in the

149

sense that, if our analysis goes far enough, we cannot imagine even the vaguest film of tint and shade without such mental 'concepts' as 'space' and 'before and after' and so on, or the 'concepts' without the film.

Your 'forms' come much later, when mind and sense seem to change places, and sense, not intellect, to give objectivity. *Demon est Deus inversus.* But metaphysics are no theme for a letter though the maledictions and beatitudes they inspire, being more compressed, are.

Your world despises Spengler because it writes for or reads *The New Statesman* and *The Nation* which have their roots in mere whirling air if he is right, but Wyndham Lewis dislikes him because he suspects him—rightly—of taking over from Bergson certain convictions, a belief in the 'datum' in fact, which commit him to 'the eternal flux.'

I too quarrel with this element in Spengler, which your *New Statesman* friends would like could they read him at all, but I think him profound and salutary for all that. There are no doubt errors of historical detail but his vast enlargement of Henry Adams's *History as Phase*, for that is what his work is, is, if it were nothing more, magnificent as a work of imagination.

Yours ever

W. B. YEATS

You might return this cutting that I may stick it into my copy of *The Logic.*

126

[after 9th April 1929]

My dear Yeats,

You are certainly quite wrong about my philosophy and I suspect you of being equally wrong about your own. Mine is in no sense bound up with science: my brother's first exploits were the absolute smashing of philosophies raised on science. He has since (and is recognised in Germany and France to have) pointed out fundamental errors in the logic of both Kant and Hegel. The European tradition to which he belongs begins with Socrates and Zeno and ends with Hume, Kant, Wittgenstein.

·A philosophical question is one that cannot be answered absolutely, and philosophers fall into different camps by temperament more than by anything else. All their answers are necessarily tentative. But their technique is too difficult for me and I believe also for you.

I begin by saying that my book is merely practical, not philosophical. 'What then do you mean by the assertion that these propositions are true?' is the kind of question my brother has discussed all his life. To which he gives many different answers according to the different categories into which he distinguishes propositions claiming to be true. I imagine, though I am not certain, that Macran has already been proved to be wrong in his assertion. 'A philosophy that leaves in any respect . . . a datum something . . . not anticipated by reason is putting us off' etc. To talk about physical science shutting up shop because it perceives that a spectator and a background are always implied in and abstracted from its descriptions (Eddington's view) is merely not to understand. For of course philosophers ignore what has already been done quite as easily as poets do.[1] Wittgenstein became a mystic by following out my brother's logic and I believe my brother is still undecided as to whether he committed some fundamental error or not. In any case, your identification of his views with those of Spencer etc. is quite absurd. Most of his work is in articles in the *Dictionary of Philosophical Terms* and consists in defining their various meanings.

Speaking personally, I cannot see in what way any thought can be considered as an ultimate; the concepts implied in it are exactly on a par with those implied in perceptions though

---

[1] Professor Moore comments that the remainder of this paragraph should be disregarded, as it is untrue.

absolutely distinct from those. (See also the appendix D in my book—page 199.) Thought implies a thinker and a thing thought about, and a thinker and an object of thought imply all the perceptions of experience. There are self-evident truths of which the truth is implied in the statement, like 'two and two make four,' and of this kind are the truths of geometry. To state them clearly is to prove them. But we cannot be certain what concepts are implied in thinking just as we cannot be certain what concepts are implied in perceiving; any that we suppose implied, as behind thought, identity, personality, continuity, eternity, etc. are both *as known and as unknown* as those implied in perceptions, space, time, diversity, etc. It is the poor philosophers not the rich who pretend to answer such questions absolutely, of which last, apparently, your Macran is one. Such people are more advanced than materialists or empiricists and science as popularly understood as an answer to philosophical propositions, but they have not an idea of the real contest between philosophers.

Of course philosophers are always trying to answer such questions and in their moments of 'personal hopefulness' imagine that they actually have answered them: that is how it comes about that they mislead their disciples. Your temperament inclines you to metaphysics and hypothetical systems. I have some leaning in that direction but my main anxiety is to remain central, not to lean very far towards any extreme. You hug conclusions and let the proof look after itself, or accept it on authority. I am always suspicious of a conclusion and incline to demand credentials both from proofs and authority. Yet both of us are ready to make practical judgements of value; we could not be poets without this readiness.

As to Spengler, Ricketts and Flint, both having read him, held him cheap, as well as W. Lewis. I do not know what *The New Statesman* said. I disbelieve in the very aim of his treatment of history. For me history ought to be science and obviously cannot be, therefore it is best when it becomes a work of art and tries to prove nothing but merely to be interesting or even beautiful.

Your sort of philosophy, I suspect, should do the same, and then it would delight me. Plato was soundest when most an artist.

About psychic phenomena I try to maintain an open mind, and should incline to reject any system which left no room for them, as many scientists do, but I think it is an hypothesis that will explain them and harmonise with other provinces of knowledge that is required, and the absence of one accounts for the evidence for them not being seriously treated.

There, I have written at greater length than I intended.

With many thanks

Yours ever

T. S. MOORE

127

Via Americhe 12-8, Rapallo.

17th April [*1929*]

My dear Sturge Moore,

No, I never compared your brother to Herbert Spencer, nor did I accuse him of an adulterous commerce with physical science. However we belong to different troupes. I can no more expect you to acknowledge virtue in Hegel than Ezra Pound to acknowledge it in Tennyson. I give up your ebullient generation, and turn to The Bright Young People who never even quarrel with a marriage partner unless they have seen somebody they like better.

Ezra Pound has just been in. He says 'Spengler is a Wells who has founded himself on German scholarship instead of English journalism.' He is sunk in Frobenius, Spengler's German source, and finds him a most interesting person. Frobenius originated the idea that cultures, including arts and sciences, arise out of races, express those races as if they were fruit and leaves in a pre-

153

ordained order, and perish with them; and the two main symbols, that of the Cavern and that of the Boundless. He proved from his logic, some German told Ezra, that a certain civilisation must have once existed at a certain spot in Africa, and then went and dug it up. He proves his case all through by African research. I cannot read German and so must get him second-hand.

He has confirmed a conception I have had for many years, a conception that has freed me from British liberalism and all its dreams. The one heroic sanction is that of the last battle of the Norse Gods, of a gay struggle without hope. Long ago I used to puzzle Maud Gonne by always avowing ultimate defeat as a test. Our literary movement would be worthless but for its defeat. Science is the criticism of Myth. There would be no Darwin had there been no Book of Genesis, no electron but for the Greek atomic myth; and when the criticism is finished there is not even a drift of ashes on the pyre. Sexual desire dies because every touch consumes the Myth, and yet a Myth that cannot be so consumed becomes a spectre.

I am reading William Morris with great delight, and what a protection to my delight it is to know that in spite of all his loose writing I need not be jealous for him. He is the end, as Chaucer was the end in his day, Dante in his, incoherent Blake in his. There is no improvement: only a series of sudden fires, each though fainter as necessary as the one before it. We free ourselves from obsession that we may be nothing. The last kiss is given to the void.

Yours ever

W. B. YEATS

I cannot spell today. I find I do not know what words contain repeated letters and what words do not. It is a matter of nerves with me. If I get out a dictionary I will have to look up too many words.

I shall be in London at the Savile in a fortnight. I want you to come and dine.

154

128

40 Well Walk, Hampstead, London.

1st May 1929

Dear Yeats,

Alas, my temperature was up again last night for no visible reason, and the Surgeon who did my operation whom I saw again a few days back said I must not think of going out till it had been normal for two days. So I fear there is no chance of my being fit on Friday.

I should very much like to see you if you could come here for tea some day, but my wife cannot manage an evening invitation while I am still invalid.

It is quite close (six minutes) from the Hampstead Tube. On issuing you turn down to the left and then take the first on your left, Flask Walk, which ends in Well Walk, and number 40 is about six houses beyond The Wells Hotel.

You might get A. J. A. Symons to take you to Ricketts. Shannon has been removed to a nursing home and R. thinks he is ever so slightly improving.

Drop us a p.c. as to which afternoon we may expect you. You might come to Belsize Park Tube, the station before Hampstead, where there is a taxi-rank a few steps above the station.

Hoping you will come,

Yours ever

T. S. MOORE

129*

Coole Park, Gort, Co. Galway.

31st August [31 July 1929]

My dear Sturge Moore,

How is Shannon? I have not heard this long time. And how is your own health?

I have been here for a couple of weeks but go to Dublin

Monday next. I am writing the last pages of my new *Vision* with a great sense of a burden thrown off. I shall within a month be back at verse again.

They are rehearsing my *Fighting of the Waves* in Dublin—a version of my *Only Jealousy of Emer* adapted to an ordinary stage. George Antheil has made strange and very exciting music for it. There are masks by a Dutch sculptor. I always feel that my work is not drama but the ritual of a lost faith. So is some of yours. I remember the solemn effect of all the early ritual part of that dance play of yours—all that with the horned figure.

Yours ever

W. B. YEATS

130*

40 Well Walk, Hampstead, London.

[*after 31st July 1929*]

My dear Yeats,

I was very glad to see your handwriting as I had no address for you or I should have written before to say that I had read the German number of the *Literary Supplement* with great interest.

Shannon is better physically, better than ever before, and very slowly, bit by bit, his mental powers seem to return. I saw him yesterday but I doubt if he recognised me, though he spoke in a way sensibly; yet his thoughts are unrelated with events.

He even criticises pictures but does not know who they are by, even his own. He set to work to copy one of his own drawings quite in the right way, but as he had not the right pair of spectacles nor a proper paper, and only a pencil instead of chalk, he could have scarcely succeeded better. There is a horrible difference in all his resemblances to what he used to be, but apparently it diminishes little by little.

I am quite well since our holiday in the Cotswolds. I am very interested by what you tell one of *Fighting the Waves* and hope it may be performed in London so that we may see it.

156

A musician named Napier Miles has asked me to write a libretto on the theme of Demeter. I can not find out whether he is really a good musician or not. All musical people seem to have heard of him and to suppose him to be good but not very good and yet not to be sure or to know.

I agree with you that the effect of masks is surprising. In my *Psyche* the effect of the white mask was astounding. All the characters wore masks in it, and even those who could not follow the words were greatly impressed by the dignity and solemnity of the effect.

Yours ever

T. STURGE MOORE

131

40 Well Walk, Hampstead, London.

15th November 1929

Dear Yeats,

Philosophical Logic[1] by L. Wittgenstein (International Library of Psychology and Philosophy. Kegan Paul, Trench, Trubner & Co.) is the book.

There is no indication of the binder in Ricketts's book so I am writing to a friend who I think will know.

These are the lines of Flecker's which I spoke about:—

> *'Had I the power*
> *To Midas given of old*
> *To touch a flower*
> *And leave its petals gold,*
> *I then might touch thy face,*
> *Delightful boy,*
> *And leave a metal grace*
> *A graven joy.*

[1] *Tractatus Logico-Philosophicus* is the correct title.

> *Thus would I slay—*
> *Ah! desperate device!—*
> *The vital day*
> *That trembles in thine eyes,*
> *And let the red lips close*
> *Which sang so well*
> *And drive away the rose*
> *To leave a shell.'*

It is called *A Queen's Song.*

I think you would like *Goodbye, Stranger* best of the Stella Bensons: it introduces a fairy-changeling in modern life in a very successful way. I should like to hear what you think of it.

With many thanks for the very pleasant evening I had yesterday, and best wishes for your convalescence and journey,

Yours ever

T. STURGE MOORE

132

40 Well Walk, Hampstead, London.

18th November 1929

Dear Yeats,

My friend Percy Smith writes that Mr. T. Harrison of H. T. Wood and Co., 18 Upper Rathbone Place, W. 1, is an excellent bookbinder whose charges are very reasonable.

He will let you know later who bound Ricketts's book but I thought you would be glad to get settled at once if this Harrison names a reasonable figure.

There is an excellent article, though too long, on criticism in *Life and Letters* for this month. The quotations are extremely well chosen. It would make very wholesome reading for Ezra. It is really witty and signed F. L. Lucas.

Yours ever

T. S. MOORE

133*

40 Well Walk, Hampstead, London.

20th March 1930

My dear Yeats,

I enclose a notice of a performance of my *Medea* though I suppose you will not be returning in time to be present, and though I am in great doubt whether this will reach you as I have no assurance that you are still at the same address. I have been much alarmed to hear vague and uncertain rumours of your having been very ill; whether these refer to the haemorrhage you had here in London or to something that has happened since you reached Rapallo I could not be certain. Please give me news.

In February there was a performance of a new version of my *Niobe*, six speakers behind a curtain, which was fairly successful. We gave two consecutive performances, one after the other, as it only plays for fifteen minutes with a five minute interval, and people all expressed approval of this plan and liked the second performance much better. It also was in itself very superior. It certainly makes people more attentive to the words.

Hoping to hear that you are as well as can be hoped and have not had to suffer,

Yours ever

T. STURGE MOORE

P.S. Tagore will be in England in May and June.

134

Via Americhe 12-8, Rapallo.

7th April 1930

My dear Sturge Moore,

Your kind and anxious letter came a little while back, and I did not reply at once because I have hardly taken up again my letter writing. I have dictated some half a dozen in all since I was ill. However the last few days I have got so much better that I hope soon to resume all my old habits.

I have been ill for five months—Malta Fever, a form of malaria, most of the time—but for some time now have been convalescent and for the last few days have been working every morning a little. However dont think of me as having been miserable. If I have been I do not remember it for the worst days have been blotted from my memory. I have managed to entertain myself, my chief anxiety the ever-increasing difficulty of finding a detective story I have not read. I am told that for ten days I read nothing, but they are blotted out, and then for weeks all serious reading was forbidden, but latterly I read daily Swift's *Letters* and his *Journal to Stella*. I have had the further entertainment of growing a beard and had for a time a magnificent appearance with the beard and hair of St. Peter out of a Raphael cartoon, and after that the local barber called every week and after several weeks produced a masterpiece, and I have now hair brushed upward and a small beard running down into a point. I am a mid-European conspirator or perhaps an Austrian diplomat and begin to think I could almost keep a secret. Probably however before I see you I shall have removed the beard for domestic reasons.

You have not seen my play at Hammersmith, nor I yours, for Hampstead and Rapallo are too far off. Mine was nothing in itself but the accessories magnificent and the method worth thinking over.

Yours ever

W. B. YEATS

I am told that during delirium—temperature 105—I dictated a letter to George Moore telling him to eat much salt because it is the symbol of eternity.

135

40 Well Walk, Hampstead, London.

16th April 1930

My dear Yeats,

I was exceedingly glad to receive your letter last night, so cheery and full of zest in tone. I am glad that your worst sufferings are forgotten and that you are now enjoying a luxurious convalescence. Convalescence is always a sort of renewed childhood, with the refreshing discovery of returning powers and the indulgence it wins on all hands.

I saw your *Fighting with the Waves* [sic] at Hammersmith and greatly enjoyed it. The masks though needlessly grotesque were full of imagination and very effective. It was a pity that the dresses had not been designed by the same artist; they were not good enough. Though I am no connoisseur I like the music and felt it was truly dramatic. The only part of it which I felt was unworthy was the song for the first lyric: neither the singer nor the music for that seemed to have the faintest notion how beautiful the words, which they made inaudible, were.

But the great moment was the entrance and dance of Fand and her mask; even her costume, though funny, was far the best. The grouping of the waves with her had real invention though their dresses were commonplace and timid. This group dancing and the music were the only parts of the performance really on a level with your words. The prejudice against masks is astonishing. I thought that every word that was not sung had been delivered too like a notice and was, if anything, over-audible, but several people have complained to me that they could not hear because of the masks. Evidently to see a mask is enough to dull some people's ears.

The invention of the dance for the fight with the waves in the beginning was not on the same level as that in the Fand dances. It was what any one would have thought of.

I think the form of the whole is good and might serve in other cases. It was far and away the most interesting and *for an artist* instructive item of the afternoon. And I was extremely interested and thrilled.

My *Medea* did not go at all so well. Not so well as at one time I hoped, but it was impossible to arrange enough general rehearsals with amateurs never free at the same times, and it was a very ragged performance. Besides, the lighting had not a sufficient range and the chief costume was ruined in being carried out. That and most of the others were only refurbishings of old costumes. Had I the range of lighting at the Hammersmith theatre at least the picture would have been first rate. The nymph's costume, the only entirely new one, was almost good though it had suffered from undue economy: still it looked extremely well. The mask for the curtain-bearer had been remade but not so much improved as my design had given me ground to hope. Still I gained a good deal of knowledge about practical matters. And some of the speaking was really good, though more so at rehearsals than at the performances. Amateur actors always fall back on their original resources and forget what has been taught them when they are behind the footlights.

Have you read Santayana's *Platonism and the Spiritual Life*? He thinks the Indian philosophers the most spiritual, but his arguments leave me sceptical as to whether mere liberation from existence has any value or probability as a consummation. I prefer with Wittgenstein, whom I dont understand, to think that nothing at all can be said about ultimates, or reality in an ultimate sense. Anyway I can say nothing that approaches giving me satisfaction, nor am I satisfied by what others say. Your *Sailing to Byzantium*, magnificent as the first three stanzas are, lets me down in the fourth, as such a goldsmith's bird is as much nature as a man's body, especially if it only sings like Homer and Shakespeare of what is past or passing or to come to Lords and Ladies.

With best wishes for your full recovery and return in good health to the North.

Yours ever

T. STURGE MOORE

136*

Coole Park, Gort, Co. Galway.

September 26th [*1930*]

My dear Sturge Moore,

I am bringing out a book of verse which I propose to call *The Winding Stair*, and I want you to make the cover design. My wife will send you typed copies of some of the contents, as this may suggest something to you. The Winding Stair, as you will see by one of the poems, is the winding stone stair of Ballylee enlarged in a symbol, but you may not think the stair, even when a mere symbol, pictorial. It might be a mere gyre—Blake's design of Jacob's ladder—with figures, little figures. I cannot send the book to press until I know the date of several publications of poems in various places, and so cannot let you have a dummy copy at present. I think it will be the same thickness as *The Tower*, and will certainly be the same as *The Tower* in height and breadth. If you cannot get a good design on The Winding Stair idea I might change the name of the book, but prefer not. Of course a suggestion of a stone stair might be possible—a hooded figure coming or going, perhaps just entering, a mere suggestion of stairs.

Yours

W. B. YEATS

137*

Coole Park, Gort, Co. Galway.

September 27th [*1930*]

My dear Sturge Moore,

I find that somebody has used the title *The Winding Stair*. I may have to change it. Do nothing for a day or two.

Yours ever

W. B. YEATS

138*

Coole Park, Gort, Co. Galway.

October 4th [1930]

My dear Sturge Moore,

Yes, I have decided to call the book *Byzantium*. I enclose the poem, from which the name is taken, hoping that it may suggest symbolism for the cover. The poem originates from a criticism of yours. You objected to the last verse of *Sailing to Byzantium* because a bird made by a goldsmith was just as natural as anything else. That showed me that the idea needed exposition. Gongs were used in the Byzantine church.

Yours ever

W. B. YEATS

I wrote the poem last spring: the first thing I wrote after my illness.

139*

40 Well Walk, Hampstead, London.

5th October 1930

My dear Yeats,

Many thanks for your various missives and for your initial poem for *Byzantium*, for which I hope to find a good design. There are one or two illegible words.

In the last stanza

> '*Marbles of the dancing floor*
> *Break* (word I cant read) *bleak aimless complexity*'

and in the penultimate stanza the first line

> '*At midnight on the Emperor's* (word I cant read) *flits.*'

Is your dolphin to be so large that the whole of humanity can ride on its back?

But there seem to be a good number of possible graphic images.

I was glad to hear from Wyndham Lewis that you seemed quite well once more during your passage through London. I suppose you may soon be returning towards the South.

Yours ever

T. S. MOORE

P.S. Please [give] my kind remembrances to Lady Gregory.

140*

Coole Park, Gort, Co. Galway.

Wednesday [*8th October 1930*]

My dear Sturge Moore,
    The lines in the last stanza which you cannot read are

> '*Marbles of the dancing floor*
> *Break bitter furies of complexity.*'

(Improvement on what I sent.)

The other line runs

> '*At midnight on the Emperor's pavement flits.*'

One dolphin, one man. Do you know Raphael's statue of the Dolphin carrying one of the Holy Innocents to Heaven?

Yours ever

W. B. YEATS

I approve Wyndham Lewis's philosophic attack in his *Apes*: indeed I always approve his philosophy.

Yours ever

W. B. YEATS

My wife is at Ballylee where my youngsters grow tall.

141

40 Well Walk, Hampstead, London.

24th October 1930

My dear Yeats,

I had hoped to have given you news of a design before this but have been in bed with 'flu that instead of passing has several times begun again. So I have not continued the design as I wish to be at my best when it crystallises.

I am not sure what the positive tenets of Wyndham Lewis's philosophy are, but I more or less understand the negative ones, and only deplore the necessity he feels of turning them into a kind of politics in which personal animosity plays a large part. But many of the situations in his *Apes* are magnificent inventions and much of the writing is most compelling.

Hoping that you and all yours are well, with kindest greetings,

Yours

T. STURGE MOORE

142

42 Fitzwilliam Square, Dublin.

5th January [1931]

My dear Sturge Moore,

There will be delay over *Byzantium.* Macmillan proposes to bring out an *édition de luxe* of all my works, including it, before the edition with your cover comes out. This will follow after one month. I say I shall have my work in *édition de luxe* finished in time for autumnal publication. Macmillan says I wont. His general knowledge of authors may be sounder than my particular knowledge of myself.

What book of your brother's should I read? I meet an old

pupil of his, O'Connell, priest and free state soldier, and our talks lack clarity.

Yours ever

W. B. YEATS

143

40 Well Walk, Hampstead, London.

11th January 1931

My dear Yeats,

All right: I understand that the cover will not be wanted for near upon a year. I will only take it up when I feel inclined.

My brother has only published three books:—

> *Principia Ethica*
> *Ethics* (in the Home University Library)
> *Philosophical Studies* (Kegan Paul & Trench)

He has contributed a good many papers to the *Dictionary of Philosophy* and to *Mind* etc.[1]

Wyndham Lewis, who has been to Germany, tells me that the Hitlerites will certainly come in to power soon and that the first law they will pass is to condemn to capital punishment whoever takes more than 5 per cent. on his invested money. Any Hitlerite who is found carrying arms is turned out of the party. The Communists, the party most opposed to them, are armed to a man and conflicts constantly occur in the streets of Berlin in which Hitlerites are shot by Communists, whom the police tend to favour as the Government fears the Hitlerites more immediately, though every now and then they raid the Communist lairs. The enthusiasm of the Hitlerites is unbelievable and they celebrate their martyrs in war songs which they sing with delirious gusto. They will denounce the Versailles Treaty and legislate against Jews. They are chiefly students and

[1] Professor Moore has contributed far more to the publications of The Aristotelian Society than to either of these.

intellectuals. They believe in property but not in rank or royalty and seem to be a refreshing crowd.[1]

Yours ever

T. STURGE MOORE

144*

Coole Park, Gort, Co. Galway.

13th October [*1931*]

My dear Sturge Moore,

I know what a blow Ricketts's death must be to you. I, though he was less to me than to you, feel that one of the lights that lit my dark house is gone. There should be some adequate study of his life, with plentiful reproductions, early woodcuts, bronzes, pictures, all. I wish I thought you were to do it. He was in our tradition its last great representative.

What has that Indian done? I heard from his friend Durga Das that he had written much of his autobiography and that it was good. Have you seen it? It will want revision. Are you doing that? I would help if it was too great a task for one. I shall be spending much time this winter here, as Lady Gregory is very infirm and old and the family have asked me to do so. I am taking up various light tasks after my day's work is done. I am now revising a volume of translations from Gaelic for the Cuala Press.

Yours ever

W. B. YEATS

[1] Sturge Moore was always opposed to totalitarianism: nothing was more foreign to his gentle nature than violence, nothing more alien to his ranging mind than loss of liberty. But in politics he had none of the scientific attitude displayed in his philosophical enquiries. He was a political idealist and, at this early stage, on hearsay, from a distance, he was prepared to like the idea of a movement composed of students and intellectuals singing songs and forbidden to carry arms. As a political prophet he was uncertain, too, and in 1922 (Letter No. 40) foretold the immediate collapse of De Valera.

145*

Coole Park, Gort, Co. Galway.

22nd October [1931]

My dear Sturge Moore,

I am sorry about the Swami but I cannot help. I am even more tied than you are. Lady Gregory's family have asked me to stay here and look after her and I have consented to do so for old sake's sake and out of gratitude for all the past. I shall be here for months, going to Dublin for a week now and again, or my wife coming here. Lady Gregory is getting gradually worse, I think, but a nursing home in Dublin would be misery to her.

Probably next Spring I shall get to London for my usual visit to see old friends. I go to Dublin for a week in November to arrange matters in connection with my theatre—the company is in America but there is a school of dancing that needs attention. Then my wife comes here that I may dictate from MSS a mass of work wanted by Macmillan. I wonder is there anybody with a love for the East and a sense of English, some woman perhaps, who could handle the Swami.

I am delighted that you shall be the official biographer of Ricketts. I shall hope for reproductions of the first Sphinx drawings, or one or two of them, of a painting called *The Wise and Foolish Virgins* and other things that I have longed to possess. Where now is his *Portrait of Mr. W. H.*? It was said to have turned up in America.

Yours ever

W. B. YEATS

146

Coole Park, Gort, Co. Galway.

25th October [1931]

My dear Sturge Moore,

Shall I sound A.E. (George Russell) on the subject? He has a passion for the East and is known to Tagore and Gandhi. I must go to Dublin in a few days to look after the school of dancing. Durga Das who saw the Swami's work thought it 'fascinating' but in need of revision. Of course it will be much better if you do it and you must put a lot of work into it as it is.

Get Hone and Rossi's *Berkeley* if you subscribe to some library; it is a fine book and I think I have done a fine introduction. It is in part Irish polemics aimed at fools and bigots at home but for all that it is, I am certain, the best Berkeley there is.

Yours ever

W. B. YEATS

The Swami should give first objective narrative and only when that is complete his doctrine. In Europe we have ideas and believe none of them because we lack spiritual experience. He has that.

147*

Coole Park, Gort, Co. Galway.

Tuesday [*1st December* (?) *1931*]

My dear Sturge Moore,

As my visit to Dublin was delayed until November 9th I thought it better to send your letter to A.E. He writes that he cannot do the work and that he has written you so. I think you must get a young man who would do the work for the sake of writing an introduction and getting his name known. There are plenty such young men in London. I might find one in Dublin but that would take time and my man when I had found him would be less efficient, through less practice, and probably have the Irish Republic in his guts. Middleton Murry might know somebody but I dont know Murry and you probably do not either. All sorts of religions interest him.

Yours ever

W. B. YEATS

148*

My dear Yeats,

Many thanks for your letter, which takes a great weight off my mind. Of course you must not expect the remainder to be as interesting as the chapters you have just read, though I think it will answer most if not all of your questions. Swami is very prudent and afraid of the English public and so reserves some of his miracles and revelations as making too strong a demand on our credulity. But your letter will help to break down this reserve. I would not even desire to write the introduction myself. The lines you describe for yours are exactly what I should desire and you are pre-eminently the right person.

I hope that now Swami can make his arrangements for America and, when I have been through the last third, filling it out with concrete anecdotes and details with him, that he will consent to leave all the arrangements for publishing etc. in my hands and find it in proof when he returns, or at any rate nearing that condition.

We were glad to learn that Lady Gregory is still well enough to read to herself with enjoyment.

I have copied out nearly the whole of your letter for Swami, and know that it will fill his eyes with tears of gratitude and thanks to Lord Dattatreya. It is an unheard of thing for a Swami to write such a book, and against all their ideas of propriety. Only Swami believes himself to have reached a stage of religious development when it is his duty to act as though he were above or quite freed from all creeds, caste, religious observance, or other formal or pre-ordained limitations: he acts on direct orders given him personally, not by tradition or custom or written laws.

A lady whom I interviewed as a possible help would not have anything to do with it as she considered the very idea of such a book would appear a sacrilege to the spiritual teachers and true Swamis she had met and learnt from in India.

One of the turning-points in his practice of concentration is when he attains the power of stopping the stream of ideas and impressions and keeping his consciousness entirely blank for longer and longer periods. That prepared him to receive more direct revelations.

With many many thanks for your kind promise of an introduction and of good offices in regard to Macmillan, and best wishes to Lady Gregory and yourself, in which my wife joins,

Yours ever

T. STURGE MOORE

149

The Corner House, Freshwater Bay, The Isle of Wight.

29th May 1932

My dear Yeats,

I only received by the weekly papers sent on from Well Walk news of Lady Gregory's death, and feel for you in this loss which however foreseen must needs be sorrowful.

She had been your fellow and mainstay in all your labours for Ireland and the Theatre for nearing forty years, and, though they were in the main crowned with success, to lose such a comrade must needs be a heavy blow, though it come peacefully and in the course of nature as I trust was the case.

Hoping that you are in good health and not too oppressed by the business occasioned, with deep sympathy.

Yours ever

THOMAS STURGE MOORE

P.S. I am away here with my wife taking our holiday early in hopes of restoring her health.

150

42 Fitzwilliam Square, Dublin.

4th June [*1932*]

My dear Sturge Moore,

Yes, the blow has been heavy. I feel that never again dare I see that neighbourhood which is so full of memories.

I have suggested to Putnams—I am some sort of literary executor—that the autobiography which Lady Gregory left ready for publication, after such condensation as the publisher demanded, should be first published. (It comes down to 1918.) Could you do the work now if on examination you find that it can be done in two or three weeks? I know the book and I think it requires very little except cutting out and a few explanatory sentences. I could not do that work because I cannot see the book with a detached mind. I think (now that I have seen for the first time some descriptions of the materials) the later part can be best done here in Dublin, and by some Irishman. For it will have to be made up out of letters, diaries, etc. It is more important historically perhaps, for it deals with the Black and Tan period, but it will require perhaps more writing, and I think much Irish knowledge. I cannot however judge till all the material is in my hands.

Yours ever

W. B. YEATS

The Agreement for *The Indian Monk* has been signed. The book is to be out early in September.

I am very sorry to hear that your wife has been ill and I hope the holiday will put all right.

151*

The Corner House, Freshwater Bay, The Isle of Wight.

[*before 9th June 1932*]

My dear Yeats,

Ricketts's work has not materialised yet, so please send me Lady Gregory's autobiography at once that I may look it over and see if I think I can do anything worth doing to it. But I cant give it my whole time as I have Michael Field work on hand, as well as my fourth volume, and at any moment proofs of the third may arrive and then I should have to stop.

Would Austin Clarke do for the later years? I like him and we might be able to work together and at such work if people can agree at all two are better than one. I merely make the suggestion. He is I believe something of a scholar both of the Classics and of old Irish literature and scholarship is always useful if it doesn't get in the way.

*   *   *

I quite understand how you feel about never seeing those places again but after some years when memory gives more pleasure than pain you will probably have the opposite feeling and it is well to look forward to that.

Yours ever

T. S. MOORE

9th June 1932

I thought this had been posted three or four days ago so please send the Life to 40 Well Walk, not here, as it would arrive too late.

152

42 Fitzwilliam Square, Dublin.

12th June 1932

My dear Sturge Moore,

I have suggested to Putnams that they send you Lady Gregory's autobiography down to 1918. This merely requires, in my belief, condensation in the earlier part. Huntingdon of Putnams gave this as his verdict and I am inclined to agree with him. However you will be able to judge when you get the typescript. I have suggested the holding over for the present of the diaries etc. or, if Huntingdon wants them at once, his sending them to me that I ɪnay read them. Until I have done that I dont feel that I can give an opinion as to the editorship.

*   *   *

I find by a codicil to Lady Gregory's will that there are various cases of letters which should probably be published. I shall have to read these. She has made me responsible for what is or is not to be published.

Yours ever

W. B. YEATS

153

42 Fitzwilliam Square, Dublin.

5th July [1932]

Dear Sturge Moore,
     Have you read Lady Gregory's autobiography and what do you think? There is unedited material of probably greater importance which could be added or published separately.

*   *   *

If the new material were treated separately I could probably get Lennox Robinson to go at it, but Huntingdon will probably want it to enliven the autobiography.

Yours ever

W. B. YEATS

Still no sign of the Swami's proofs. He got the typed copy back to work on it again.

175

154*

Riversdale, Willbrook, Rathfarnham, Dublin.

6th September 1932

Dear Sturge Moore,

I have been looking through your correspondence. Some time in July you wrote to me saying that you thought Lady Gregory's autobiography should not be condensed in the early part. You had not, however, when you wrote, read the whole manuscript. I would be greatly obliged if you will tell me what your final judgement was. I have to see the Gregory lawyer in a few days and want to give him a general account of things.

I think my Academy of Letters will be launched in about a week. I am lecturing on the 18th and want to have the announcement and the names before then that I may have a few enemies to answer.

We shall meet in London in October. I am going to lecture in America to advertise the Abbey Players who will be there, and I shall pass through London.

Yours ever

W. B. YEATS

155

Savile Club, 69 Brook Street, W.1.

June 4th [1933]

My dear Sturge Moore,

I am over again as they are giving me an Honorary Degree at Cambridge on the 8th and I am reading my poems tomorrow to the English Club at Oxford. All more or less legitimate forms of self-advertisement.

I am giving a birthday party to myself on June 13th at the Savile Club—8 o'clock. Do please come. Black tie.

Yours ever

W. B. YEATS

156*

Riversdale, Willbrook, Rathfarnham, Dublin.

7th September [*1933*]

Dear Sturge Moore,

I am grateful to you for that fine cover. It is one of the best you have done. Were it in gold it would, I think, equal that for *The Tower* though I know there are some that prefer blue to gold.

For a year now I have written little but prose, trying for new foundations.

Yours ever

W. B. YEATS

157

40 Well Walk, Hampstead, London.

10th June 1934

My dear Yeats,

Ricketts in his journals mentions having written a long letter to Lady Gregory after Lane's death—an appreciation of him, for which she thanked him very warmly.

I wonder if you have come across this letter and would allow me to publish it in association with the journals. This need in no way clash with any other use you might wish to make of it.

Have you any other letters of Ricketts's of general interest? I should greatly like to see them if you have, and would have them copied and returned to you if you were so good as to send them.

Yours ever

T. STURGE MOORE

158*

40 Well Walk, Hampstead, London.

18th July 1934

My dear Yeats,

Many thanks for your letter. I am ordering the book.

I do not know either the name or address of Lady Gregory's daughter-in-law so cannot write to her to ask for the letter about Hugh Lane and any others there might be. Would you kindly send me her name and address?

The local papers confirmed what my wife had heard and in part seen, that Father Vincent McNabb knelt down and kissed the Anglican Bishop of Willesden's feet *in contrition* for the sins against justice and truth of the Romish Church: he had referred to Galileo etc.[1]

Yours ever

THOMAS STURGE MOORE

159

Riversdale, Willbrook, Rathfarnham, Dublin.

24th July 1934

Dear Sturge Moore,

I have now been through the file and I send you, under separate cover, registered, all the Ricketts letters I can find. I have not read them through and so cannot tell what importance they have.

---

[1] *The Hampstead and Highgate Express* of 7th June 1934 describes a demonstration arranged by the Christian Churches of Hampstead in support of the League of Nations, when the celebrated Father said that until there was religious peace there could not be world peace, and that every Christian community was to blame for having caused warfare; he then performed this act of contrition 'for such crimes as had been committed by the Roman Catholic Church.'

Sturge Moore's design for the cover of *The Winding Stair*

We put that wardrobe you made a design for the embroidered doors of a few years ago into my son's room. I was in the room yesterday and found it more beautiful than my memory of it. It has now got the exactly right surroundings. I had not seen it for some years as it was among the things we left in Italy.

Yours ever

W. B. YEATS

160

c/o B. J. Fletcher, Daneway, Sapperton, Cirencester.

2nd August 1934

Dear Yeats,

Many thanks for yours of the 24th and for the nice things you say about my cupboard. It was an experiment and owes all its practical success to the workmanship of Ethel Pye which was wonderfully ingenious. I am exceedingly glad you find it wear so well and still able to please.

I hoped to the last to receive the C. R. letters which you said you were sending under separate cover but they had not arrived when we left home yesterday. If they have not started when this reaches you please address them as above: we shall be here till the 15th. You forgot to give me the name of Lady Gregory's daughter-in-law and her address so that I may write to her for C. R.'s letters, especially that about Lane written shortly after this latter's death.

Hoping to hear from you soon,

Yours ever

THOMAS STURGE MOORE

161*

Riversdale, Willbrook, Rathfarnham, Dublin.

8th August [1934]

Dear Sturge Moore,

I have mislaid your last letter and so must write to Hampstead. The day before the letter came the Ricketts letters had gone to Hampstead.

Mrs. Gough's address is 'The Abbey, Celbridge, Co. Kildare, Ireland.'

I have had a dramatic success with *The Resurrection* and a dance play *The King of the Great Clock Tower.*

[no end]

162*

40 Well Walk, Hampstead, London.

7th December 1934

My dear Yeats,

I am returning the letters of C. R., which you so kindly lent me, enclosed with this.

I find that Lady Gregory says in a letter to him that the letter about Lane which so pleased her had been addressed to you but that you had given it to her. I wrote to her daughter-in-law to the address that you sent me in August but have had no reply, but I asked her for a letter to Lady Gregory about Lane, not one addressed to you which had been given to Lady Gregory.

Who is Ruth Shine who is mentioned in connection with Lane's disappearance? Is she a married sister of Lane's?

Is 'Shains' the Irish for Saints or merely a mis-spelling of C. R.'s? 'The Well of Shains' he writes, meaning Synge's 'Well of the Saints'?

Hoping you are well and working. (I have been indulging in

whooping cough. It seems after sixty you become liable once more, so you should run no avoidable risks.)

With many thanks for the letters,

Yours ever

THOMAS STURGE MOORE

163*

Riversdale, Willbrook, Rathfarnham, Dublin.

12th July [*1935*]

Dear Sturge Moore,

I thank you for the Rossetti drawing and the money gift—from you and others—John Masefield brought.

I am sunk in my *Cambridge Book of Modern Verse*. So far as Michael Field is concerned I shall probably follow the guidance of your preface. Dorothy Wellesley and Eleanor Wylie are so far my chief excitements for both are new to me. My period is from the death of Tennyson; this enables me to put Hopkins among the Victorians.

Yours ever

W. B. YEATS

164*

40 Well Walk, Hampstead, London.

8th December 1936

My dear Yeats,

I was very glad to receive your *Modern Verse* this morning, though vexed that my wife's letter should have been sent on to you. (No, the Oxford Press sent no official copy.) She had corresponded only with the Oxford Press before and had no idea that you would be troubled or that the non-appearance of the book was anything but a clerk's oversight. I had wished that no mention should be made of the cheque but as in the conditions sent them before this had been mentioned I let it stand. Pray forgive us for this unseemliness.

I had left the question of what I should receive entirely to you as I understood you had a fixed sum and did not at all know how it would divide up, especially as one or two poets had made exorbitant demands. I shall be wholly content with whatever falls to me in the general division. Also in respect of Michael Field pay me at the same rate as the majority.

I have not yet had time to more than glance through the book and introduction but am delighted to find so much that is new to me and that seems of high quality. Your introduction is full of persuasive charm and interesting ideas and I feel sure the book will be a great success in spite of the wrath of what Ricketts called 'Little London,' which sets the fashions and supposes that it is followed much more than it really is. Of course I looked for several favourites in vain, but that was inevitable, and as far as I can yet judge you seem to me to have been most consistent and independent, and nobody should demand more.

I was very interested to hear your wireless talk, and was so shocked by its abrupt end that I imagined that you had been cut off in the middle of a sentence. I wrote to *The Times*, but they said they would only publish my letter after I had written to the B.B.C. My conviction was increased when Riette met [*a friend*] who told her that what had been cut off was 'It cost me a damned lot of hard work to put that into poetry *and the* ——— *has been and taken it all out.*' But the B.B.C. most politely persuaded me that this last phrase had not been in your MS.[1]

I hope your health is improving. I heard you had been hardly

[1] Yeats's broadcast talk on Modern Poetry ended with a plea that poetry should be read as poetry, rhythmically, and not as prose, and the last sentence of his talk (as printed in *The Listener* of 14th October 1936) was the quotation of William Morris's remark after hearing an unsatisfactory reading or recital of *Sigurd the Volsung*: 'It cost me a lot of damned hard work to get that thing into verse.'

able to see anyone while in London and spent most of the time at Lady Gerald Wellesley's in Sussex.

Pater's *Gioconda* reads splendidly as a poem and makes an excellent commencement.

I congratulate you, and remain,

Ever yours

T. STURGE MOORE

165*

40 Well Walk, Hampstead, London.

Dear Yeats,   *22nd March 1937*

I have been meaning to write to you, and now seize the opportunity while I am waiting to be fetched to poor Shannon's funeral.

I think

'Silence Sings'	volume I	p. 7
'Desire Sings'	,, ,,	p. 79
'The Rowers' Chant'	,, ,,	p. 192

These three have all attracted musicians before, as among the children's poems, 'The Little School,' have

'Wind's Work'	volume I	p. 141
'Lullaby'	,, ,,	p. 150
'Water'	,, ,,	p. 171

I myself believe that

'Reason Enough' (first 8 lines only)	volume I	p. 71
'Summer Lightning' (last 9 lines only)	,, ,,	p. 69
'Pan's Prophecy' (first 8 lines only)	,, III	p. 93

would all make good songs, and among the children's poems

'Goathooves'	volume I	p. 145
'Hands'	,, ,,	p. 156
'Shoes and Stockings Off'	,, ,,	p. 151

I have not seen any of your broadsheets so do not know what public is addressed and have kept to things that can be and ought to be chanted even without music.

'Light Heart'	volume I	p. 13
'O Wonder of the Sea' (song only)	„ IV	p. 224
'Song without Rhymes'	„ III	p. 242
Also first 8 lines on p. 135	„ IV	

sing themselves but are perhaps more special in the public addressed.

The books you asked me to let you know the titles of are:—
Jungle Tide (about Ceylon) by John Still (publisher Blackwood). *Low Company* (written by a convict) Mark Benny (published by Peter Davies).

I have a feeling you asked me also for someone's address or something but memory fails me.

Hoping that you are keeping well and enjoying life as much as may be,

Yours ever

T. STURGE MOORE

I have just remembered it was R. Bridges's *Triolet* which is 17, last number in his first *Book of Shorter Poems*. First line 'All women born are so perverse.'

NOTES

LETTER NO. 1

Sturge Moore's *Aphrodite against Artemis* was published by The Unicorn Press in 1901. It was performed by The Literary Theatre Society in 1906, with Florence Farr as Phaedra and Gwendolen Bishop as Aphrodite and with scenery and costumes by Charles Ricketts, and gave rise to a lively controversy started by William Archer, who was shocked because in the scene in which Phaedra tries to seduce her stepson he replies to her incestuous advances by telling her to 'Get up!'

Sturge Moore's play about Herod was *Mariamne*, published in 1911 by Duckworth.

Yeats's play about Cuchullin was *On Baile's Strand*, and his poem *Baile and Aillinn*.

LETTER NO. 2

Diarmuid and Grania by George Moore and W. B. Yeats was produced on 21st October 1901 at the Gaiety Theatre, Dublin, with Mrs. Benson as Grania. It was not performed in England.

LETTER NO. 4

The plays were probably *Cathleen ni Houlihan, The Pot of Broth* and *The Hour-Glass*, which, with Lady Gregory's *Twentyfive* and Fred Ryan's *The Laying of the Foundations*, were performed on 2nd May 1903 at the Queen's Gate Hall, South Kensington.

Sturge Moore's 'company' was The Literary Theatre Society, whose reading of *Aphrodite against Artemis* in circumstances similar to those described here by Yeats gave Charles Ricketts so much amusement.

LETTER NO. 5

The Hour-Glass was produced by the Irish National Theatre on 14th March 1903 at the Molesworth Hall, Dublin. It is not recorded that Sturge Moore designed the setting and costumes but Yeats must have asked his advice about them.

At this time Sturge Moore was living at No. 20 Fitzroy Street, Selwyn Image's Hobby Horse House. Image, who as a young man had been ordained, was by then a professional artist: he designed stained-glass windows and wrote poetry, and in 1910 became the Slade Professor of Fine Art at Oxford.

LETTER NO. 6

Yeats must also have asked Sturge Moore's advice on the costumes and setting for *The Shadowy Waters*, produced on 14th January 1904 at the Molesworth Hall.

Wagner's period is not a convenient one to define: Yeats's figure is illegible and may be 5 or even 13.

The Vale Shakespeare was published 1900-1903, edited by Sturge Moore, who had also edited for the Vale Press *The Passionate Pilgrim* and *The Songs in Shakespeare's Plays* (1896) and *Shakespeare's Sonnets* (1899).

The meeting was of The Masquers, founded in March 1903 to give performances of plays, masques, ballets and ceremonies but lasting only a few months. Yeats and Sturge Moore were members.

LETTER NO. 7

Adolphe Appia (1862-1928), Gordon Craig's counterpart on the Continent, was Marie Sturge Moore's first cousin. The book referred to by Yeats is either *La mise en scène du drame wagnérien* (1895) or *Musik und Inszenierung* (1899).

Salomé had been produced in 1905 at the Bijou Theatre, Bayswater, by the New Stage Club (semi-amateur) but not *A Florentine Tragedy*, of which Robert Ross said that Wilde had characteristically finished what he never begun, so that Sturge Moore, at Ross's request, wrote an opening scene of some 250 lines. The play was acted by Gwendolen Bishop (Bianca), Reginald Owen (Guido Bardi) and George Singleton (Simone). Shortly afterwards Puccini telegraphed for the text, as he thought of writing music for it.

LETTER No. 8

Yeats's *Poems 1899-1905* were published in October 1906 and included new versions of three plays.

The passage on page 160 criticised by Sturge Moore comes towards the end of *Baile and Aillinn*.

LETTER No. 9

Yeats's *Deirdre* was first performed at the Abbey Theatre on 24th November 1906, with Frank Fay and Miss Darragh. It was published in 1907.

The domestic event in the Sturge Moores' household was the birth of their daughter.

LETTER No. 10

In *The Academy* of 15th June 1907 W. Teignmouth Shore, the journalist, reviewed performances given in London by the Abbey Theatre of Synge's *The Playboy of the Western World* and Lady Gregory's *Spreading the News*. Shore deplored Synge's subject, and, though he applauded the soundness and wisdom of the Abbey Theatre's aims, he ended by saying 'Whether or not Mr. W. B. Yeats is the right man to hold the helm is another matter into which we have not at present space to enquire.' The words 'every article' in the latter should probably read 'a very [*adjective omitted*] article.'

Laurence Binyon's *Attila* was produced at His Majesty's Theatre on 4th September 1907 by Oscar Asche, who took the title rôle. Charles Ricketts designed the costumes and scenery.

The comedy was George Fitzmaurice's *The Country Dressmaker*, performed at the Abbey Theatre on 3rd October 1907, so that Yeats's 'three days' is only approximate.

The tragic farce was *The Unicorn from the Stars*, produced at the Abbey Theatre on 21st November 1907.

LETTER NO. 12

Yeats worked on *The Player Queen* for many years. Mrs. Patrick Campbell read it in 1909. It was first played by the Stage Society at the King's Hall, Covent Garden, on 25th and 27th May 1919, with Edith Evans as Nona, Gwen Richardson as the Queen and Maire O'Neill as Decima. The Abbey Theatre production, on 9th December 1919, was with May Craig, Shena Tyreconnell and Christine Hayden.

Sturge Moore's letter, to which this is a reply, is lost. See POSTCARD, NO. 30 below.

LETTER NO. 13

Sturge Moore's *Kindness* was included in the volume *Theseus, Medea and Lyrics*, Duckworth 1904.

Sturge Moore's *The Vinedresser and Other Poems* was published by The Unicorn Press in 1899.

Yeats was a member of The Rhymers' Club, founded in 1891.

LETTER NO. 16

The thirty original members of The Academic Committee of The Royal Society of Literature were Alfred Austen, Laurence Binyon, A. C. Benson, A. C. Bradley, Robert Bridges, S. H. Butcher, Joseph Conrad, W. J. Courthope, Austin Dobson, James George Frazer, Edmund Gosse, Viscount Haldane, Thomas Hardy, Maurice Hewlett, Henry James, William Paton Ker, Andrew Lang, Sir Alfred Comyn Lyall, John William Mackail, T. Sturge Moore, Viscount Morley, George Gilbert Murray, Henry Newbolt, Edward Henry Pember, Sir Arthur Wing Pinero, George Walter Prothero, Walter Raleigh, G. M. Trevelyan, A. W. Verrall and W. B. Yeats. Dr. Percy W. Ames was Secretary.

The first meeting was held on 10th April 1911, when Lord Haldane in his inaugural address said it would be the function of the Committee 'to attend to the standard of style in this country.... Style means form. Form and matter are never wholly separable.'

LETTER NO. 19

Shaw was made a member of The Academic Committee, as were also J. M. Barrie and Lady Ritchie. George Wyndham had been elected shortly after the original thirty members.

LETTER No. 20

Gitanjali by Rabindranath Tagore was published by The India Society in 1912 and by Macmillans in 1913. Yeats who wrote the introduction had helped Tagore to learn English.

The Source is No. 61 and *On the Sea Shore* is No. 60. It would be interesting to know the changes that Sturge Moore suggested, and the one change that Yeats approved, but no copy has been found with the changes marked and Sturge Moore's letter about them has been lost.

The following was written by Sturge Moore on the back of Yeats's letter: it is not known whether such a letter was sent. 'My dear Yeats, You strain at gnats and swallow camels. What Tagore and I so object to in the version you call "yours" is the use of "flits" which means nothing, being quite wrong, and the arrangement of the phrases, which is absurdly un-English and clumsy. I thought you would notice these things at once and jump at them but you only worry over a phrase which can have no harmony while it is set in a dislocated sentence. However it is too late to convert your blindness.

Yours ever, T. S. Moore.'

LETTER No. 21

Yeats first asked Sturge Moore to design a cover for one of his books at the end of 1915. Between then and 1940 Sturge Moore designed the covers for twelve books, the last coming out after Yeats's death in 1939.

1916 *Reveries* (a figure in a half-open door)
1916 *Responsibilities* (a tree and a hawk)
1918 *Per Amica Silentia Lunae* (a rose)
1919 *The Wild Swans at Coole* (three swans, one in a circle)
1919 *The Cutting of an Agate* (a mask)
1921 *Selected Poems* (like *Reveries* but much more complex) published in America only
1921 *Four Plays for Dancers* (two masks)
1921 *Four Years* (an eagle attacking a small bird)
1928 *The Tower* (a tower)
1933 *The Winding Stair* (stairs and a figure on a dolphin)

1934 *Letters to The New Island* (swans and masks) published in
America only

1940 *Last Poems and Plays* (a figure supporting a globe and standing
on a lion)

Most of these books were published in Ireland by the Cuala Press,
and in America and England by Macmillan. Sturge Moore's designs
are generally on the English and American editions only, but there are
exceptions and full particulars of all the editions are to be found in
Mr. Allan Wade's *Bibliography of Yeats*.

LETTER NO. 22

Le Mystère de la Charité de Jeanne d'Arc by Charles Péguy.

LETTER NO. 24

The Rose design was almost certainly that for *Per Amica Silentia
Lunae* written in 1917 and published in January 1918. So this letter
must belong to the summer of 1917 in spite of certain inconclusive
evidence suggesting that it might have been written in summer 1916
before No. 22.

The wardrobe had fine silk panels, designed by Sturge Moore and
embroidered in silk and beads by Miss Ethel Pye, depicting a young
girl riding on a unicorn among steep mountains.

A lady recently described to the editor a ceremony she went through
on her first visit to Woburn Place. 'Who is the unknown coming to
me out of the darkness?' was the challenge, and the lady who was
either more lively or less impressionable than some, endeavoured not
to smile at the prosaic nature of her reply. She was conducted solemnly
to the bedroom, where she and the poet sat one at each end of the bed
and contemplated the cupboard (presumed to contain the poet's
clothes).

LETTER NO. 25

More than two years earlier, in 1915, Sturge Moore had made a
design to illustrate Yeats's line 'the Infinite Fold' which Yeats wanted
to have embroidered as a table centre for Mrs. Shakespeare.

LETTER NO. 26

The block was for Mrs. Yeats's bookplate.

The castle was Thoor Ballylee, bought by Yeats in June 1917.

POSTCARD, No. 30

Yeats *was* at No. 73 St. Stephen's Green. Sturge Moore's letter is lost, but Yeats's letter No. 12 may belong to 1919, coming after letter No. 31.

See note to Letter No. 12 about *The Player Queen*.

LETTER No. 31

Anne Yeats was born on 24th February 1919.

A lively controversy on prosody was started by Sturge Moore's letter in *The Times Literary Supplement* of 9th January 1919.

LETTER No. 32

The design chosen for *Four Years* was an eagle attacking a small bird. The candle in waves comes in Yeats's bookplate.

LETTER No. 33

The cover was for *Four Plays for Dancers*, and had a design of two masks and a hawk with outspread wings.

LETTER No. 34

Michael Yeats was born in August 1921.

LETTER No. 36

Sturge Moore's *To Leonardo da Vinci* was published in the volume entitled *The Unknown Known and a Dozen Odd Poems* (Martin Secker, The Richards Press, 1939).

The engraving referred to was done on soft wood with the grain showing through, like a Japanese print, and represented sphinx-like statues or daemons seated in the desert. It was used by the Sturge Moores as a Christmas card.

LETTER No. 41

Sturge Moore's *Medea* was produced at Steep in July 1923. Letter No. 42 and a letter from Yeats to Mrs. Sturge Moore suggest that Yeats may have seen it, in spite of what he says here. Miss Hilda Thompson was Medea.

The philosophy book was *A Vision*.

LETTER No. 43

Sturge Moore's *Judas* was published by Grant Richards in 1923.

LETTER NO. 49

In April or May 1924 Ricketts and Shannon moved from 'the Palace'—Lansdowne House, Holland Park, built by Sir Edmund Davis so that Ricketts and Shannon could live on the top floor, where they had splendid rooms and studios full of precious and beautiful things, and a view of London right round the compass—to 'the Castle' as Yeats calls Townsend House, St. John's Wood, a charming house now unfortunately destroyed.

LETTER NO. 50

Villiers de l'Isle Adam's *Axel*, translated by H. P. R. Finberg, was published by Jarrolds in 1925.

LETTER NO. 51

The big book that had been preoccupying Yeats was *A Vision*.

LETTER NO. 54

It may have been Mrs. Olivia Shakespeare who saw the vision. *The Refutation of Idealism*, by G. E. Moore (in *Mind*, October 1903).

LETTER NO. 58

Ruskin, like other people in similar circumstances recorded by Harris in his autobiography, and like the cat, was not himself on this occasion.

LETTER NO. 59

Professor Moore suggests that the fourth sentence in the second paragraph should read 'we are only quarrelling about a word, not about a fact.' The MS. is quite clear, however, and the meaning seems to be that if Yeats thinks there *are* snakes on the counterpane and Sturge Moore does not then the quarrel is about the acceptance of the original fact (of the snakes' existence) or about the definition of hallucination (in the form of snakes) rather than about a general theory of philosophy.

N   193

LETTER No. 61

Yeats refers to the review of Professor William Pepperell Montague's *The Ways of Knowing*, to be found on page 4, column 3 of *The Times Literary Supplement* of 4th February 1926.

LETTER No. 63

Sturge Moore's *Armour for Aphrodite* was published early in 1929. Or, the reference may be to a study of Paul Valéry entitled *A Poet and His Technique*, published in *The New Criterion* of June and October 1926.

LETTER No. 65

A Defence of Common Sense by Professor Moore was published in J. H. Muirhead's *Contemporary British Philosophy*, second series, in 1925.

LETTER No. 66

Professor A. E. Heath, writing on 'Realism in Modern Thought' in *The Encyclopaedia of Religion and Ethics*, refers to William James's *Essays in Radical Empiricism* (1912).

LETTER No. 69

Casey's play was *The Plough and the Stars*, acted at the Abbey Theatre on 8th February 1926.

LETTER No. 71

The passages quoted by Yeats just before his signature and in the postscript came from Chapter IV and Chapter III respectively of Whitehead's *Science and the Modern World*.

LETTER No. 77

This letter may belong to 16th June 1927 coming after letter No. 88, but in No. 76 Yeats implies his intention of looking up certain passages in Professor Moore's essay.

LETTER No. 78

This letter answers Yeats's letter No. 76, and also No. 77 which arrived while Sturge Moore was writing No. 78.

LETTER NO. 83

Yeats's three preceding letters are No. 77 of 16th June, No. 79 of 23rd June and No. 81 of 25th June. Either a letter from Yeats is missing or Sturge Moore forgot that he had already answered letter No. 77. Yeats's fourth letter No. 82 of 26th June arrived on 30th June.

LETTER NO. 84

There is a gap of nearly a year between this letter from Yeats and the last one from Sturge Moore. It is not known whether any letters are lost.

LETTER NO. 86

Yeats's letter, which is typewritten, has the sculptor's name as Van Loo: Mrs. Yeats has corrected this slip.

Shelah Richards, one of Ireland's best and most accomplished actresses, and much admired by Yeats for her dramatic gifts, was very young at the time of this scene. She did not suffer from her family, but she did wish temporarily to break a contract with the Abbey Theatre in order to play in *The Plough and the Stars* in America, and as she did this, returning to the Abbey Theatre almost a year later, she must have persuaded Yeats, and not *vice versa* as he had hoped.

LETTER NO. 87

Two letters must be missing before this: one from Sturge Moore sending *The Tower* and bookplate designs, and one from Yeats praising the bookplate and continuing the philosophical argument which is taken up by Sturge Moore in the next letter.

The Only Jealousy of Emer was performed in Holland a year or more before it was performed at the Abbey Theatre in the revised form of *Fighting the Waves* on 13th August 1929.

LETTER NO. 88

Sturge Moore refers Yeats to page 208 and later to pages 200-205 of *A Defence of Common Sense*: see note to Letter No. 77.

LETTER NO. 89

Anne's bookplate was never finished, though there are further references to it in later letters.

Unless the two men met, there must have been between this and No. 88 at least one letter from Sturge Moore, enclosing the bookplate, and another from Yeats explaining what he took to be 'essentials.'

LETTER NO. 91

This letter is wrongly dated. No doubt Sturge Moore was distracted by the move from Steep back to Well Walk.

LETTER NO. 92

'That bald-pate' was Bertrand Russell, whose hair was always enviably profuse and is, of later years, admirably silver. Mrs. Yeats told Joseph Hone that the reference was to II Kings 2. 23, 'go up, thou bald-head.'

Wyndham Lewis's new or last book, referred to in this and the following letters, was *Time and Western Man*. It was published in 1927, as were *The Lion and The Fox*, *The Childermass* and *The Wild Body*. *The Art of Being Ruled* was published in 1926.

LETTER NO. 94

Presumably No. 91 and No. 92 are the relevant letters.

LETTER NO. 95

Sturge Moore had forgotten that in Yeats's letter No. 84 and his own No. 85 it was clearly arranged that he should do a frontispiece.

LETTER NO. 101

A letter from Yeats must be missing before this. He seems to have hoped Sturge Moore had re-drawn Anne's bookplate.

In *The Times Literary Supplement* of 10th May 1928 Sturge Moore reviewed Evelyn Waugh's *Rossetti: His Life and Works*.

LETTER NO. 103

Sturge Moore's adaptation of Mallarmé's *Le Cygne* was printed in *The Fortnightly Review*, 1st, October 1930. This fact and the considerations mentioned in the note to the following letter No. 104 suggest about June 1928 for the two letters.

LETTER NO. 104

Yeats's reference to his 'instructors' suggests that he was writing *A Packet for Ezra Pound*, first published by the Cuala Press in June 1929. His statement that he would not publish for at least twelve months gives the date of this letter as June 1928 approximately.

The letters cannot belong to the period of *A Vision*, when Yeats also was in communication with his 'instructors,' and before Sturge Moore left Well Walk, that is about 1918, because the Savile Club moved to Brook Street on 1st November 1927.

LETTER NO. 105

Sturge Moore was designing a label on which Yeats could write his name and a line of verse and give it to his friends to stick in their copies of his works.

LETTER NO. 109

The Collected Works of Yeats (Macmillan) have a cover designed by Charles Ricketts and a unicorn, also designed by him, inside the front and back covers.

LETTER NO. 116

In 1926 Yeats had been appointed Chairman of the Committee set up to advise on the new coinage for Ireland. He had thought of designs by Carl Milles but those chosen were by Percy Metcalfe and represented birds, beasts and fish.

LETTER NO. 117

Yeats refers here to Swift's own Epitaph, carved in Latin on a stone in the floor of St. Patrick's Cathedral, Dublin. Yeats translated it in *The Winding Stair*, and there is another version by him in Lady Gregory's *Journals*.

LETTER NO. 118

Life and Letters, February 1929, contained *The Closing Door* written by Sturge Moore in memory of Henry Poole, R.A.

About the middle of January 1929, Charles Shannon had the accident from which he never recovered though he lived till 1937: he fell on the marble staircase at Townsend House while hanging pictures. Sturge Moore used to say that the friendship between Ricketts and Shannon was the most marvellous human relationship that had come within his observation. There is no doubt that Ricketts's comparatively early death in 1931 was due largely to the sorrow brought on him by Shannon's tragic state of mind.

LETTER NO. 119

The lyric that Yeats was so pleased with was *Three Things*, published in *Words for Music Perhaps*, 1932.

LETTER NO. 121

Sturge Moore's definition of beauty in the words quoted by Yeats has not been traced, but page 21 of *Hark to These Three* may have given rise to Yeats's thoughts.

LETTER NO. 122

Sturge Moore's *Armour for Aphrodite* (Grant Richards and Humphrey Toulmin, The Cayme Press, 1929) had a cover designed by himself in red and white and green showing the Goddess emerging from her bath and wearing, apparently, a fireman's helmet and cricket pads.

Professor S. Alexander's essay on *Art and Material* is discussed in Appendix C of the book.

LETTER NO. 123

The four lines of Swift come from *The Progress of Beauty*.

LETTER NO. 124

Beyond the Threshold by Jean Paul Raymond (Charles Ricketts) was printed privately in 1929.

Armour for Aphrodite was reviewed in *The Times Literary Supplement* of 4th April 1929.

LETTER NO. 125

The book reviewed was Macran's *Hegel's Logic of World and Idea*.

LETTER NO. 129

This letter must have been written before 13th August, when *Fighting the Waves* was produced by the Abbey Theatre, so 31st August cannot be the right date.

The horned figure was in Sturge Moore's *Medea*.

LETTER NO. 130

Psyche in Hades was performed in 1927 at Sir Thomas Legge's house Fair Rising, Steep, with Lady Legge as Psyche.

LETTER NO. 133

Medea was performed on 31st March and 1st April 1930, at the Rudolf Steiner Hall, with *Meleager* by Robert Trevelyan. The editor has vivid memories of the dress-rehearsal. Passages of great poetic beauty were interrupted by sudden comic events: some of the conversations between the poet and the electrician were almost worthy of being incorporated in the text; two of the actresses arrived so late that the poet's wife was heard distraughtly murmuring as a refrain below the verse 'J'aurai *cru* qu'elles auraient *pu* arriver à temps'; and it was reported that the leading lady's 'bun' had fallen into the fire-bucket just before her entry. Many of the problems were solved by the cleverness and kindness of Miss Hetty Moore, the poet's sister, and the two performances, in spite of the criticisms made by Sturge Moore in letter No. 135, must have remained in the memories of many of the audience as rare and satisfying experiences. Mrs. Wheeler took the chief parts in *Medea* and in *Meleager*, and Riette Sturge Moore and Sylvia Legge were also in the cast.

Niobe was performed in February 1930 at Mrs. Wheeler's house with Mrs. Wheeler as Niobe.

LETTER NO. 136

This letter has two slight sketches by Yeats of Jacob's Ladder and Ballylee stairs.

LETTER NO. 137

The book was eventually published as *The Winding Stair* though it is referred to as *Byzantium* in most of the letters.

LETTER NO. 138

The lyric *Byzantium* was written in the spring of 1930, after Yeats's illness, and as a result of Sturge Moore's criticism of the last verse of *Sailing to Byzantium*, made in his letter No. 135 of 16th April.

Byzantium first appeared in *Words for Music Perhaps* (Cuala Press, 1932), where it is incorrectly dated 1929: it is dated 1930 in *The Winding Stair*, in *The Collected Poems* and in *The Definitive Edition*.

LETTER NO. 139

This letter cannot have been written on 5th October if letter No. 138 was correctly dated 4th October.

LETTER NO. 140

Wyndham Lewis's *The Apes of God*, published in 1930.

LETTER NO. 144

An Indian Monk: His Life and Adventures, by Shri Purohit Swami, was published by Macmillan in 1932 with an introduction by Yeats, who had sent the Swami to Sturge Moore, 'one of our finest critics.'

LETTER NO. 145

Sturge Moore wrote an Introduction to *Charles Ricketts, R.A.: 65 Illustrations* (Cassell, 1933), and also compiled *Self-Portrait: Letters and Journals of Charles Ricketts* (edited by C. Lewis: Peter Davies, 1939), but he had hoped that time and circumstances would have allowed him to produce a more important Life, written on a really comprehensive scale, of the man whom he and all his friends regarded with so much admiration.

LETTER NO. 147

Sturge Moore's letter referred to here is lost; it is likely too that Sturge Moore wrote an answer to Yeats's letter No. 144 which is missing.

LETTER NO. 148

Yeats's letter referred to here is also lost.

LETTER No. 151

Sturge Moore was working on the Michael Fields' Journals, and published *Works and Days* (John Murray) in 1933.

The Collected Edition of his poems came out in four volumes in 1931-1933, published by Macmillan.

LETTER No. 154

The letter written by Sturge Moore in July is lost.

The formation of The Irish Academy of Letters was publicly announced on 18th September 1932. The project had taken shape in discussions between Yeats and George Russell at Lady Gregory's house. Bernard Shaw, Lennox Robinson and Lawrence of Arabia were among those who became members, and George Moore and James Joyce among those who refused to do so.

LETTER No. 156

The cover was for *The Winding Stair*.

LETTER No. 158

A letter from Yeats is missing before this one, so it is not possible to say which book is referred to.

LETTER No. 161

The Resurrection and *The King of the Great Clock Tower* were played at the Abbey Theatre on 30th July 1934.

LETTER No. 162

Charles Ricketts, like Thackeray, was an artist in spelling.

LETTER No. 163

John Masefield and Desmond MacCarthy had gone over to Ireland on the occasion of Yeats's seventieth birthday. Sturge Moore was ill and could not go.

Cambridge Book of Verse is of course a joke. Sturge Moore wrote the Preface to *A Selection from the Poems of Michael Field* (The Poetry Book Shop 1923).

LETTER NO. 164

Pater's description of La Giaconda from *The Renaissance* is called *Mona Lisa* in Yeats's anthology.

LETTER NO. 165

During 1935 the Cuala Press issued monthly Broadsides, new and old songs edited by Yeats and F. R. Higgins. Sturge Moore's poems were never published in this form, though The Poetry Bookshop published as their Rhyme Sheet No. 6 his *Beautiful Meals* and *Water*, with decorations by himself, twopence coloured, penny plain.

INDEX

INDEX

INDEX

For Product Safety Concerns and Information please contact our EU
representative GPSR@taylorandfrancis.com
Taylor & Francis Verlag GmbH, Kaufingerstraße 24, 80331 München, Germany

www.ingramcontent.com/pod-product-compliance
Lightning Source LLC
Chambersburg PA
CBHW071521110726
47908CB00003B/909